HARD
TIME

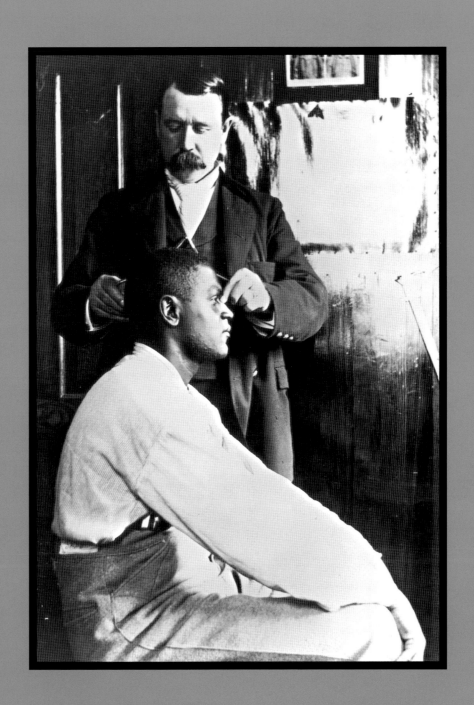

HARD TIME

Voices from a State Prison, 1849–1914

Edited by Ted Genoways
Foreword by Ted Conover
Introduction by James Taylor Dunn

MINNESOTA HISTORICAL SOCIETY PRESS

ST. PAUL

Acknowledgments: Sincere thanks to researchers Ben Petry and Chris Taylor; Bob Horton, Peter Latner, Kevin Morrissey, Eric Mortenson, Adam Scher, Debbie Sher, and Duane Swanson, all of the Minnesota Historical Society; Brent Peterson of the Washington County Historical Society, Stillwater; Penny Petersen, for information on Nellie Sullivan; and James Taylor Dunn, whose landmark essay on the prison, originally published in *Minnesota History*, has stood the test of time.

---

www.mnhs.org/mhspress

Design and typesetting: Percolator

Printed in China by Pettit Network, Inc., Afton, MN

10 9 8 7 6 5 4 3 2 1

International Standard Book Number
ISBN 0-87351-433-5 (cloth)
ISBN 0-87351-434-3 (paper)

♾ The paper used in this publication meets the minimum requirements of the American National Standard for Information Sciences—Permanence for Printed Library Materials, ANSI Z39.48-1984.

Library of Congress Cataloging-in-Publication Data available upon request.

Contents

Foreword

TED CONOVER

THIS BOOK ARRIVES LIKE A KNOCK on the door from a long-forgotten relative. Prisons, after all, are like a family's unpleasant secret—that no-good son we'd rather not talk about, that embarrassing incident best forgotten, symbols of the prisoner's failure and of ours. Who would have thought that records as rich as these even existed? Or that somebody would dream to assemble them in such an appealing and accessible way? The chorus of first-person voices and the gallery of official photographs show that, for all of its unpleasantness, prison is a remarkable world and was, if anything, even more interesting way back when.

In *Hard Time* you will find one black inmate telling off another in the pages of the prison newspaper; the words of an agonized female prisoner after she learns her six-year-old son has died of diphtheria; prisoners confessing in detail to the savage beating of a guard; a photograph of a different guard, blinded in one eye by a prisoner's knife, who, years later, bears no grudge against his attacker; and the unforgettable description by a light-fingered Englishman of the prison band in which he served as clarinetist:

> The quality of prison music is not choice: it droppeth as a foretaste of purgatorial hail upon the unwilling ear. But . . . I owe too large a proportion of what little remains of my sanity to this same concerted conspiracy against artistic canons to condemn it utterly.

The uniforms, the mug shots, the stance of the guards and the stanchions buttressing the old wooden prison walls tell a story of a faraway place that we created and then forgot, of a demolished prison brought back to life.

Some of these voices echo eerily in the present. Walter Turner, confined to a dark cell for eleven days, informs his fellow convicts that "There is just two classes of men who can stand the hole. They are those who have full control over their minds and those who were practically born in holes," which strikes me as true. Good prison officials try to convince those on the outside that some men deserve a second chance, and bad prison officials succumb to the many opportunities that prison still offers for corruption and self-enrichment. Even at the old Stillwater, the growth in prisoner numbers swelled the buildings to overfull, inmates committed suicide, solitary confinement provoked madness and hate, and criminals with clear potential for personal reform languished with nothing to do.

But what sticks with you here is the look of the men staring into a camera—many for probably the first time in their lives—for their mug shots. Perhaps because they're dead, it's easier to grant them their humanness than it is to do the same for contemporary criminals, easier (for me, anyway) to wonder about their offenses, their victims, and their backgrounds: they haven't hurt anybody we know, and will never hurt us. We see their faces and understand something about their lives; we see the roots of today's troubled prisons in the violent, deadening place called Stillwater.

Hard Time is a feast of primary sources which, because it is so personal, impresses deeply; a beautiful book that insists on the humanity of the banished.

Broken glass plate negative, from a box of miscellaneous photographs of inmates, about 1870

The Minnesota State Prison during the Stillwater Era

JAMES TAYLOR DUNN

FEW PRISONS CAN CLAIM a past as colorful as the old Minnesota State Prison at Stillwater. In its sixty-five year history, from planning to closing, the prison played host to intriguing characters and dramatic events: the capture and imprisonment of the Younger gang in 1876; the prison fire of 1884; the daring escape of Frank P. Landers and Oscar J. Carlon in 1887; the twine shop insurrection of 1899; and the manhunt for escaped convicts Peter Juhl and Jerry McCarty in 1911. Its history is packed with such peculiar characters as "Bull Beef" Webber, the warden who allowed murderers to embark on hunting trips and an incarcerated prostitute to work out of the prison hospital; Charles Price, a convicted mur-

Deputy Warden Robert M. Coles (right), 1912, at the exit to one of the prison shops with his pit bull and an unidentified man, perhaps one of the shop supervisors

derer who reformed and became famous for his prison greenhouse; and John Carter, the convicted thief turned poet who won his freedom with his verse.

The less remembered stories are here too, the stories of daily life by prisoners whose notoriety has faded: George L. Bartlett, who writes about the terrifying first days of incarceration; Azilda Beaudry, a woman convicted of murdering her husband, who writes achingly of her separation from her children as they die one by one of disease; Walter Turner, an African American inmate, who renders advice on surviving solitary confinement; and Samuel A. Phillips, who speaks frankly about sex in the prison. Their stories give voice to the forgotten history of the prison, lived not warden to warden, but day to day. As one might

1

expect, prisoners complain of bad food and over-work, boredom and claustrophobia, but they also have lucid insights into the complexity and persistence of societal ills.

THE SOMETIMES CHAOTIC EVOLUTION of the prison itself, through construction of buildings and changing wardens and different philosophies of penology, set the context for life at Stillwater. In 1849 Minnesota Territory had no prison controlled by civil authorities. In his message to the first territorial legislature on September 3, 1849, Governor Alexander Ramsey strongly advised that "there should be proper and safe places of confinement" for prisoners in the new territory, and urged the legislature to ask the federal government for money to construct a prison. One would suffice for the whole territory, the governor believed, "until the period when increased population and greater wealth, may enable each county to have a proper building for the purpose." Earlier, through an arrangement with the commandant of Fort Snelling and with officers at Fort Ripley, civilian malefactors were held under arrest at these military posts, but they frequently escaped from the territory before they could be sentenced—a situa-

tion which caused a writer for a St. Paul newspaper, the *Minnesota Chronicle and Register* of April 20, 1850, to rationalize that "probably this is the best way to dispose of our rascals so long as we are destitute of a prison."[1]

Selection of a site was the next problem. A proposal that the prison be built in the village of St. Anthony was met by a majority of its residents "with the most marked contempt," according to the *Minnesota Pioneer* of St. Paul for January 30, 1851. Another suggested location was farther up the Mississippi and more toward the middle of the state, perhaps somewhere in Benton County. But this idea was rejected by the larger downriver cities, according to the same newspaper, as too "far removed from the present and probable future center of population." In February 1851, the legislature designated St. Paul as the territorial capital and selected Stillwater, the thriving metropolis in the St. Croix Valley, as the site for the penitentiary.[2] The new prison would be erected on four acres of land in Battle Hollow, a marshy ravine near the north end of the town, close to the river. Surrounded on three sides by precipitous cliffs, Battle Hollow had received its name from a bloody encounter of Dakota and Ojibwe which took place there in July 1839.

In May 1851, after the Minnesota board of commissioners of public buildings voted to construct the prison of stone, the firm of Jesse Taylor and Company, which included Francis R. Delano, Martin Mower, and John Fisher as partners, began work. Among penitentiary buildings completed by early 1853 were a three-story prison house with six cells and two dungeons for solitary confinement, a workshop, and an office, all designed by Fisher, constructed of material taken from nearby quarries, and located within an enclosure of about 280 square feet surrounded by a twelve-foot wall. Outside was the warden's house, halfway up the south hill overlooking the prison. To manage this physical plant, the territorial legislature of 1853 provided for an administrative struc-

ture consisting of three inspectors, appointed by the governor for terms of two years, and a warden, named by the legislature for a term of five years. The law designated Delano, one of the contractors, as the first warden, and he assumed office on April 4, 1853.[3]

A native of Massachusetts, Delano had settled in Stillwater by 1851 and had there engaged with little success in lumbering. During his early years as warden, he built up a profitable private business on the prison grounds. With his own funds, he purchased and took into the government-constructed penitentiary about eight thousand dollars worth of steam-powered machinery for the manufacturing of shingles, sashes, doors, flooring, wagons, and plows. He put the prisoners to work in his shops and in addition hired some fifteen Stillwater residents to assist the convicts in filling special orders—such, for example, as fencing for the Capitol grounds in St. Paul. Regulations required that the inmates be kept busy from sunrise to sunset, with thirty minutes allowed for each meal. Conversation was never permitted. As punishment for unruly conduct or disobedience, there was first a bread-and-water diet in solitary confinement and, as a last resort, twenty lashes a day for five days.[4]

Prisoners were held at Fort Snelling before the construction of the territorial prison in Stillwater (daguerreotype, about 1850).

Security arrangements within the newly built penitentiary, however, left much to be desired, and escapes were frequent. During a ten-month period in 1856, seven men and one woman fled confinement. Their methods of escape varied. The hall floor was pried up; an iron cell door was lifted from loosened hinges; a burglar's bar was smuggled in, according to the warden's record book, by "unknown hands"; locks and shackles were picked; iron window bars were sawed; holes were dug through the outside wall.[5] A writer for the St. Croix Union of Stillwater complained on May 2, 1856, that either "the penitentiary is badly constructed or . . . some one or more of its officers are grossly derelict in duty." Delano, however, convinced the editor, Milton H. Abbott, that the fault lay not with the warden but with the prison, since the walls and buildings were not, as claimed, "of the most approved and substantial kind." The fact that there were no night guards was never mentioned.

The warden, as stipulated by law, was obliged to accept temporary prisoners from Minnesota counties that lacked adequate jail facilities. The local governments involved were, however, expected to pay all expenses incurred in confining prisoners from their areas. Although official statistics mention only five convicts received at the territorial prison between 1853 and 1858, the half-dozen usable cells were nonetheless continuously crowded with temporary county prisoners. Most of the time, two and often three men were forced to share a single unit.[6]

The counties sending prisoners to Stillwater frequently failed to pay the lodging fees, and the warden found it increasingly difficult to collect from them. By the beginning of 1857 they owed Delano

Francis R. Delano served as warden from March 1853 to March 1858 (pastel portrait by Jaeger).

seven hundred dollars, and he claimed that he had "stood all the loss he could." Following an inspection visit to Stillwater, the prison committee of the legislature recommended that the warden should not be held responsible for prisoners if the counties were lax in paying for their keep. An act to this effect was approved on May 23, 1857, and Warden Delano immediately freed prisoners from Winona, Nicollet, and Houston counties because payments were not forthcoming from the county commissioners.[7]

"There is something wrong about the Territorial Prison," reads an editorial in the *Weekly*

Pioneer and Democrat of St. Paul for November 5, 1857, published after the escape of an accused murderer from LeSueur who was placed in the Stillwater prison for safekeeping pending trial; "any person who desires it can escape from it, and the Warden does not even think it worth while to offer a reward, or notify the public." On November 21, 1857, the *St. Paul Financial, Real Estate and Railroad Advertiser* joined the fray by claiming that "a canary bird in a 10 acre field, with the bar doors down at that, would be more safely caged." Scarcely had the year 1858 begun, when a new convict, perhaps to prove this statement correct, led three of his companions in a successful jailbreak. Unobserved, they picked a large hole through the cellblock wall and, with the aid of a handy ladder, quickly cleared the inadequate exterior wall while the guard was attending church services elsewhere in the village. *The Advertiser* of December 19, 1857, expressed the opinion that "the Warden should have a fixed salary and no officers in the institution should have an interest in the contracts, or in the labor of the convicts; nor be the owner of any part of the tools or machinery used in the institution." The *Stillwater Messenger* added its bit on February 10, 1858: "Our Penitentiary is a great hum-

bug. There is no security about it—it is a cheat, a swindle, a disgrace."

As a result of all these accusations, the United States government stepped into the picture and instituted lawsuits against Michael McHale and Roswell B. Johnson, both of whom were prison officials and business partners of Delano. The territorial legislature immediately ordered a grand jury investigation, which took place late in 1857. The jury members, in reporting to Judge Charles E. Flandrau, found Warden Delano and Deputy Warden McHale "negligent and careless." A total of eight scathing indictments were brought against the prison officials for alleged neglect of duties. Delano, on the other hand, challenged the moral character of several members of the grand jury, most of them fellow townsmen. Without using any names, he accused one of "having been tried in a sister State for the highest crime known to the laws," and another of spreading his traps and dealing "a little game of Chuck-a-luck" between the sittings of the jury. Delano also complained that the jurors spent exactly twenty-seven minutes at the prison and visited only three cells. Most of their time while there was taken up by the high jinks of a Stillwater "eccentric wag" and saloon proprietor named Emanuel Dixon Farmer who was a member of the jury. For example, the jurors locked Farmer in one of the cells and released him only when he promised that he would supply drinks for everyone present.[8]

Realizing, no doubt, that the territorial laws governing the penitentiary were faulty, and aware of the need for reorganization and reformation of the prison system with the approach of statehood for Minnesota, Governor Samuel Medary was apparently loath to press charges against Delano and his deputies. During the early months of 1858 nothing more was heard of the grand jury indictments and the lawsuits were dropped. The prison's first warden remained in charge until the expiration of his term on March 4, 1858.[9]

ON THE DAY Delano retired, Colonel William C. Johnson, sheriff of Washington County and former Marine Mills justice of the peace, presented his commission as warden. Although his appointment had been signed by Governor Medary the previous November, Johnson was undoubtedly restrained from taking over until the close of Delano's term. When he did appear, Delano's deputy, McHale, who had been authorized to transact all the business of his partner, refused

to surrender the prison keys. He demanded full payment for the machinery placed within the walls by Delano and Company before allowing anyone else to take charge.[10] Johnson did not force the issue. He made no attempt to assume the position to which he had been named. Mc-

Francis D. J. Smith officially oversaw the prison from March 1858 to August 1858, while Michael McHale, deputy warden under Delano, refused to surrender control of the prison and its shops.

Hale acted as warden for another five months, though Francis D. J. Smith, chairman of the Board of Inspectors, was officially in charge of the prison while the board tried to resolve the squabble. In the meantime, Minnesota joined the galaxy of states, and its new government faced a busy period.

Not until August 19, 1858, was a new warden, acceptable to all factions, appointed. This was thirty-two-year-old Henry N. Setzer, a Stillwater lumberman and a prominent representative in the first territorial legislature. He assumed direction of the state prison after an amicable agreement was reached with the former warden and his business associates and the acting warden surrendered the keys. Setzer's first order was for six muskets and bayonets from the state armory for the use of prison guards.

Setzer immediately resolved the thorny county prisoner problem. "There is no authority now existing," ruled the new warden when he refused one such prisoner, "by which the State prison can be converted to the use of a common jail, to keep in custody persons merely committed for trial."[11] Setzer and the state board of prison inspectors also clamped down on many lax methods prevalent at the territorial penitentiary. It was decided that the state institution could be used only for business relating to the prison—for example, unauthorized persons would not be allowed to walk on the walls surrounding the buildings. During territorial times the health and spiritual needs of the inmates had been neglected. This was rectified under the new regime by the appointment in August, 1858, on a part-time basis, of Dr. Helon Fay Noyes of Stillwater as the prison's first physician and the Reverend John C. Caldwell, rector of the local Presbyterian church, as the first chaplain.[12]

A Democrat who was not amenable to the politics of Abraham Lincoln, Setzer put himself on record as being unwilling to hold office under any "Black Republican administration." Thus, in December 1859, he tendered his resignation. Before doing so, however, he touched on a subject that was to draw comment from all succeeding wardens until the old territorial penitentiary was finally abandoned in 1914 and the new Minnesota State Prison occupied at Bayport. He strongly recommended that the recently constructed prison be removed from the "marshy and unfit" location in Battle Hollow, which, he said, would never offer enough space "to enlarge and improve the State Prison to make it fit and secure enough to answer the purposes of its erection.[13]

Henry N. Setzer, warden from August 1858 to January 1860, transformed the prison into a legitimate institution by arming the guards and recruiting a prison physician and a chaplain.

John S. Proctor gave up his Stillwater hardware store to receive the prison keys from Setzer on January 16, 1860. According to the politically opposed *Stillwater Democrat*, the newly appointed warden was the "very best man whom Gov. Ramsey could have selected from the Republican ranks of this city." Proctor served well for eight years under four Minnesota governors. His long tenure of office, during a period of spoils and

great political favoritism, proved the wisdom of Ramsey's choice. At a yearly salary of $750, Proctor, according to the *Messenger* of January 30, 1866, "bro't order out of chaos which formerly adorned and gave a stench" to the institution.

Perhaps the new warden's outstanding contribution to improved organization within the state prison was a plan for reducing the length of convicts' sentences through good behavior. As originally instituted in 1862, the scheme allowed a total of three days for each month of satisfactory deportment, to be granted at the discretion of the warden. Bad conduct brought a forfeiture of credits gained. This system, considerably altered and broadened over the years, is still in effect. Early in 1874 the Minnesota legislature passed a law providing that prisoners be paid for the three days a month of reduction in sentence which they could gain under the good behavior plan. At a salary rate of forty-five cents a day, which contractors were then allowing each able-bodied prisoner, and inmate could

John S. Proctor, warden from January 1860 to February 1868, instituted the use of "penitentiary stripes" to assure that escaped convicts would be recognized.

earn for himself a maximum of a dollar and thirty-five cents a month. The total accumulated by any one man, however, could not exceed twenty-five dollars. This arrangement, according to the inspectors, was a great morale builder, for it kept the inmates from being despondent and preserved their self-respect.[14]

Another major change made by Warden Proctor was the discarding of the red and blue jackets, blanket wool caps, gray pants, and hickory-cloth shirts worn previously by the prisoners. Proctor furnished all convicts with clothing that would help make detection certain in event of escape. It consisted of hip jacket, woolen pants, and skull-cap, all with alternate black and white horizontal stripes. These "penitentiary stripes," first introduced in 1860, were not completely abolished within the prison walls until 1921. Proctor was also the first to use guards for patrolling the prison at night. During the long winter evenings, convicts were allowed to burn lamps in their cells until eight o'clock in the hope that they might get inspiration from such works as Washington Irving's *Washington*, Stephen Elliott's *Sermons*, a novel called *The Jealous Husband*, and Harriet Bishop's *Floral Home*, the only Minnesota book in the prison's small collection. Although the in-

mates' library had been started by Delano and somewhat revitalized by Proctor, there was little indication during these early years that it would later become one of the finest prison libraries in the country.[15]

IN 1859 JOHN B. STEVENS of Stillwater, a manufacturer of shingles and blinds, had leased the prison workshop from the state for five years at a rental of a hundred dollars a year. He took over all convict labor, paying a generous seventy-five cents a day for each full-time worker. This was the beginning of the contract system in the Minnesota State Prison, which ended only when the old prison was abandoned fifty-five years later. When Stevens' shingle mill unfortunately burned in January 1861, forcing the contractor into bankruptcy, George M. Seymour and his partner, William Webster, Stillwater manufacturers of flour barrels, took over the contract for prison labor. They established a wage for a day's work from each prisoner, which was scaled to advance from thirty to forty-five cents over a five-year period. Toward the end of the 1860s, Seymour joined with Dwight M. Sabin, soon to be a state and later a United States Senator, to form the new firm of Seymour, Sabin and Company. This concern continued to rent the prison shops and to employ the inmates, who worked in silence under guard, manufacturing sashes, doors, blinds, barrels and other wood products.[16]

The contract system exploited by these firms was criticized by a warden for the first time in February 1868, when Joshua L. Taylor, a St. Croix Valley lumberman, was placed at the head of the prison by Governor William R. Marshall. Both Taylor and the inspectors could read the handwriting on the wall when they urged that inmates be allowed to work for the benefit of the state rather than for private concerns. They felt that the existing system was detrimental to Minnesota's financial interests

Joshua L. Taylor, warden from February 1868 to March 1870, declared that prison labor would henceforth benefit the state, rather than private individuals

and that the evils resulting from it were "positively injurious to the discipline and hostile to the reformation of the convicts." Prisoners rose at 5:30 A.M. and worked for eleven hours in summer and nine in winter. During 1870 forty-eight prisoners produced $50,000 worth of tubs, buckets, and barrels for the steadily expanding Seymour,

Sabin and Company. In 1871 the firm's sales amounted to $135,000.[17]

Over the succeeding three years antagonism toward the contract system increased, as it became the general opinion that the institution was being managed at too great an expense to the state and too large a profit to the contractors. Newspapers of 1874 suggested that "the prison should be self-supporting by the contract system or the state should buy out the contractors and do its own business." Already criticisms were growing strong against profiteers. And the warden agreed that "the contact system of labor is bad," and that "sooner or later it must be abandoned."[18]

Such criticism of the contract system notwithstanding, Seymour, Sabin and Company continued to expand. For example, the firm began making threshing machines in 1876 and its business so prospered, especially with the introduction of the nationally known Minnesota Chief threshers, that the company soon could boast of being the world's largest manufacturer of such machines. Its net profits for 1881 came to over three hundred thousand dollars. In May, 1882, the North Western Manufacturing and Car Company was organized by Sabin and "certain wealthy persons" representing large railroad interests.

Sabin's original company was absorbed into this burgeoning concern, which continued to make doors, sashes, blinds, flour barrels, and threshers, as well as to take on the construction of portable and traction farm engines, and to manufacture freight and passenger cars for several Northwestern railroad companies.[19]

In addition to prison labor, which the company's officers openly bragged they had obtained through a "very advantageous contract" with the state, approximately twelve hundred civilians were employed in the prison shops and around the extensive yards that had mushroomed outside the walls. "It was never expected when the contract for prison labor was made," apologized the inspectors in 1884, "that the Manufacturing Co. of Seymour, Sabin & Co. would develop into the mammoth N.W. Manufacturing and Car Co. . . . Had that result been foreseen, the shop room would most certainly have been restricted, and also the number of citizen employees allowed within the prison grounds."[20]

But the company, through agreements and contracts signed with the state, had established too firm a foothold to allow any fundamental change in the existing arrangements. During their twenty-two years at the Stillwater institution, the contractors managed to assume virtually complete control over prison affairs. Almost from the beginning they alone were given the lucrative building contracts for additions, improvements, and repairs in and about the prison grounds. As a result, the money received annually by the state from Sabin's company for prison labor and rental of the workshops was considerably less than the amount the government paid out to the same firm for constructing buildings and repairing the prison wall. The contractors even assumed the right to choose guards and officers employed by the state in the prison. The evils of the contract system, first recognized by Warden Taylor, had multiplied.[21]

Eventually, in 1887, the state legislature, yielding to pressure from the St. Paul Trades and Labor Assembly, ruled against prison labor contracts that would come into competition with free enterprise. The long-standing agreement with Seymour, Sabin and Company and its successors was therefore terminated a year later, leaving over four hundred unemployed prisoners for whom only such temporary work as repairing the warden's house and finishing the prison wall could be found. Meanwhile, the car company continued to use the prison premises for its manufacturing operations.[22]

As a result of an exhaustive report on convict labor made by the inspectors in 1889, and because of the disastrous effect of idleness on prisoner morale, the legislature allowed a partial resumption of the contract system. Accordingly, the warden made arrangements for a two-year convict labor agreement with the Minnesota Thresher Company, a firm which was formed by the stockholders of the car company, and purchased its assets. Under this agreement half of the prisoners could be employed by the contractors. To furnish work for the remaining inmates, plans were formulated in 1890 for the state to go into business on its own. Since a combine of cordage manufacturers was then charging unreasonable prices for binding twine, to the disadvantage of Minnesota's farmers, a binder twine industry was initiated at Stillwater, and this proved successful almost from its beginning. Prison-made twine, sold at a reduced price, meant considerable saving to the farmers of the state, and Minnesota thereby established what was for many years the foremost state-account system in the nation. At the same time, the power wielded by the contracting company had been greatly lessened, indicating that the contract system of prison labor was on its way out.[23]

Between 1860 and 1867, the number of state prison inmates jumped from four to fifty-two—an increase due, said the board of inspectors, to the "general carnival of crime which seems to reign over the whole country." This caused overcrowding and made necessary the construction of new buildings. A three-story cellblock was erected and an additional shop built by Seymour and Webster, contractors, and paid for by the state so that Seymour and Webster, manufacturers, could employ a large number of prisoners.[24]

AT THE END of his two-year term, in 1870, Taylor declined reappointment because the salary of a thousand dollars a year was "not commensurate with the position and duties required to be performed." To replace him, Governor Horace Austin appointed Captain Alfred B. Webber of Albert Lea in March. An occasional attorney-at-law and part-time politician, best known as an ex-hotel-keeper, he was a political appointee with few qualifications for the position. His credulity was clearly displayed in his defense of a pardoned convict: "It is pretty generally believed now that he was not guilty of any crime. I know he was not, for he told me all about it after he was pardoned.[25]

Less than half a year after his appointment, Webber summarily dismissed long-time Deputy Warden Robert R. Davis on the strength of accusations of theft made by William McGee, a military prisoner. Davis countered with multiple charges against Webber, including "dereliction of duty, violation of prison discipline, and corruption in office." They were strongly denied by Webber, who scored Davis for his "inhuman and unjust treatment" of prisoners. The testimony presented to Governor Austin contained imputations that the warden, by this time nicknamed "Bull Beef" Webber, speculated for his own benefit in prison flour and beef; and that one life convict was frequently permitted temporary freedom so he could go hunting in Wisconsin. The testimony showed, however, that the prisoner's partner in most of this extracurricular activity was Deputy Warden Davis. Webber not only allowed wives to enter the prison to sleep with their husbands, but prisoner Nellie Sullivan, a popular nineteen-year-old Twin Cities prosti-

Alfred B. Webber, nicknamed "Bull Beef," served as warden from March 1870 to October 1870. In a few short months, Webber earned a reputation as the most corrupt warden in the prison's history.

tute and madam, continued to ply her trade behind the walls at Stillwater.

Governor Austin finally asked for Webber's resignation, and in September he named a Civil War general, Horatio P. Van Cleve of St. Anthony, to fill the vacancy. Van Cleve refused the senate-confirmed appointment, having "no intention of moving to Stillwater." Colonel William Pfaender of New Ulm also declined it. The choice eventually fell to another St. Croix Valley lumberman, Henry A. Jackman, a self-styled "very Black Republican," who for many years had served as a member of the prison board of inspectors.[26]

Under Warden Jackman, the first major building program interrupted the routine of prison life, as "the old dilapidated and tottering Territorial buildings" were removed. The only original building left standing was the warden's house. New and substantial accommodations for a maximum of 158 prisoners were erected in their place by the prison labor contractors. The warden called the new quarters "an honor to the State, a credit to the builders, and a blessing to the inmates." Only two years later, however, the new cellblock proved to be less of a "credit to the builders" than Warden Jackman had thought, for

faulty construction made it easy enough for a prisoner to escape by crawling under his cell door and between the window bars. Fewer than a hundred inmates were received during Jackman's tenure. Punishment consisted of confinement in the dungeon on a reduced fare, some recalcitrants being shackled with a fifty-pound ball and chain for as long as a month. Occasionally, however, there was a relaxing of discipline. Following Warden Proctor's term in the 1860s the prisoners had been granted three labor-free holidays— Thanksgiving, Christmas, and Independence Day— when they were treated to special meals. The local

Henry A. Jackman, warden from October 1870 to August 1874, leveled the territorial prison facilities and erected a new cell block that could hold up to 158 men.

newspaper reported in detail on Jackman's Fourth of July party in 1873. All work was suspended, recorded the *Stillwater Gazette* of July 8, and the inmates were allowed freedom of the buildings, but not of the yard. Cigars were distributed as a prelude to a "sumptuous dinner" at noon, which was followed by more cigars. Later in the day, "a barrel or two of lemonade was concocted and dispensed—with an unsparing hand."[27]

The year 1874, however, was a hapless one for Warden Jackman. In May, Deputy Warden Eri P. Evans, who had been relieved of his recently acquired position, retaliated by charging the warden with fraud, theft, neglect of duty, and infractions of discipline. Both the warden and inspectors demanded an immediate and thorough investigation, which resulted in the dismissal of all accusations. The governor was handed four hundred pages of testimony, but so far as is known he did not request Jackman's resignation. At about the same time, Alonzo P. Connolly, a St. Paul newspaperman, visited the prison and reported in the *St. Paul Dispatch* of June 24, 1874, that many of the newly built cells were damp and absolutely filthy, and that some of the bedding was wet. Faced with continued criticism, and "feeling keenly the effect of these charges," Jackman submitted his resignation in July 1874. Governor Cushman K. Davis appointed John A. Reed of Sterling in Blue Earth County to the post, and he became the new warden at what one newspaper called "that miserable basin."[28]

The newly constructed cell block and prison shops in an early drawing of the prison, about 1874.

WARDEN REED'S TWELVE YEARS at Stillwater were unsettled ones. The number of inmates more than quadrupled and the state found it difficult to furnish adequate living and working space as well as yard room for the convicts and for the ever-increasing number of civilians employed by Seymour, Sabin and Company. Until this time, Minnesota had without much trouble managed to expand its prison facilities to meet the slowly growing criminal population. But the 1870s saw a continuing need for enlargements to the physical plant.

Two fires in 1884 were major catastrophes for the prison. Both occurred in January, but neither appeared set by a "citizen incendiary." On January 8 the large four-story woodworking shop and several smaller buildings burned. Far more devastating was the conflagration of January 25, which started in the basement of the care company office on a bitter cold night, and raged completely out of control, leaving a great part of the prison a mass of ruins and blackened walls. With the cellblock threatened, the National Guard was called out and 350 chained prisoners were led from their smoke-filled quarters into the subzero weather. An inmate who did not obey the order to leave was the only casualty. "The striped sojourners in our city seem to have enjoyed the episode," reported the *Messenger* for February 2, "as they have been able to talk with each other quite freely, play games, and read at will."

The prison on the following day must have been a discouraging sight. There were no quarters for officers or prisoners; few provisions remained intact; and all utensils, hospital equipment, furniture, and library books were gone. About the only objects saved were the prison records. Governor Lucius F. Hubbard went immediately to consult with Warden Reed, and they decided to transport some of the prisoners to neighboring county jails, including those at St. Paul, Minneapolis, Winona, and Hastings, as well as the local Washington County lockup. The rest were housed temporarily on the prison grounds. When time came to remove the selected convicts, a vast crowd pulled and pushed and elbowed its way in front of the barred gates. "The appearance of the prisoners," said a reporter in the *Daily Globe* of St. Paul for January 27, "chained two and two, dressed in their striped clothes . . . created quite a sensation," as they

John A. Reed was warden from August 1874 to February 1887, a time that saw numerous upheavals at the prison, including the arrival of the Younger gang and the fire of 1884.

marched down the main street of Stillwater to the railway depot. Before being taken to Winona, the matron and six female inmates, three serving terms for murder, were guests of the warden and his wife at their home adjacent to the prison. When the prisoners later returned to Stillwater, it was to a temporarily roofed and fire-scarred cell block.[29]

Considerable reconstruction was completed by mid-1886, with 582 cells and ample shop room and machinery to employ over five hundred workmen. Since the prison population at the time was only 387, there was enough space for years to come. The contracting company faced financial difficulties after the fire and was

placed in the hands of a receiver. In spite of setbacks, however, all available prison labor was employed making engines and threshing machines. "Careful observation," reported the state board of corrections and charities, "has confirmed our good opinion of the administration of Warden Reed."[30]

Outside the walls, however, trouble was brewing for the warden. In their report for 1886, the three prison inspectors spoke out strongly against accusations which had been leveled at those connected with the management of the institution. "Ambitious men, disappointed, scheming demagogues," the inspectors informed Governor Hubbard a few months before he went out of office, "cannot understand why it is that business men will accept such positions as these unless it is to ally themselves to rings and assist in defrauding the State." It became more and more obvious that a change of wardens would accompany the next political shift.[31]

The change came when Andrew R. McGill became governor of Minnesota early in 1887. He did not reappoint Reed, but named in his stead Halvur G. Stordock, a farmer from Rothsay in Wilkin County. Two of the three prison inspectors resigned because of the governor's move "to

Halvur G. Stordock, warden from February 1887 to August 1889, oversaw the establishment of the *Prison Mirror*, the prison's weekly newspaper, but he became embroiled in a controversy with former Warden Reed and resigned in 1889.

make place for some of his political friends."[32] Stordock was the last warden in Minnesota appointed by a governor.

Within a few months the new warden and the inspectors demanded an investigation of what they called prison "irregularities and immoralities" under Reed. The reasons for the request are obscure. The governor appointed a committee of three from the state board of corrections and charities to study the accusations, and before they reached a decision several months later, many scandalous charges and countercharges had been advanced by Reed, Stordock, and their respective lawyers. During the hearings, Governor McGill relieved Stordock of his official responsibilities. Mrs. Sarah E. McNeal, whom ex-Warden Reed had shortly before called the "very competent matron" of the prison, was the principal witness against him. Also giving testimony were several convicts who must have spent a good part of their time trying to gather evidence (based on "vague suspicions," said the report of the investigating committee) by listening through keyholes and peering over transoms.[33] Even the *Prison Mirror*, the inmates' newspaper established by Stordock in 1887, entered the fray with biased accounts of the inquiry. On September 21 it quoted an article from the *Glencoe Register* which flatly asserted that Reed and other prison officials were "living off the state and were public plunderers." This controversial editorial policy, and the *Mirror's* original motto, "God Helps Those Who Help Themselves," were both quickly scrapped.

In December, the committee reported that none of the charges against Reed was sustained; both Warden Stordock and Mrs. McNeal were reprimanded, and Reed was gently censured. After the dismissal of the indictments, Stordock was restored to his position, but Sarah McNeal did not return as matron. This affray almost resulted in tragedy when, in June of the following year, Reed attempted suicide at his Minneapolis home.[34]

In 1889, the legislature tried to take political favoritism out of prison affairs by vesting all direction and control of the Minnesota institution in a five-member board of managers, which was made responsible for the appointment of the warden. In August 1889, John J. Randall, a sixty-year-old coal merchant from Winona, was selected to replace Stordock. "Randall has a good record," reported the *Messenger* on August 3, "and will doubtless make a good warden." But the Stillwater newspaper could not resist inferring that Senator Sabin, of the prison-contracting firm, had influenced the choice. Randall's short term of eighteen months was marked by several innovations of importance to the prison's future. The first steps were taken toward establishing a school. In 1890 a Chautauqua reading circle was organized, and this group remained an active and influential part of prison life for almost fifty years, until 1938, long after the collapse of similar experiments in the few other institutions which tried them.[35]

Once again, however, accusations from discharged prison officials were heard, following a now familiar pattern. This time the victim was Randall, who many critics considered too lenient toward the inmates. There were others who felt that Randall was being forced out because he was not amenable to the wishes of the prison contractors. "Until the position is removed from politics," advised the *Gazette* on December 4, 1890, "the life of a warden in Minnesota will continue to be an unhappy one." A committee of the House of Representatives which, in January 1891, investigated the conduct and management of the prison, concluded that both Stordock and Randall were removed "because their administrations did not meet the wishes of those connected with the prison contractors."[36] That Randall was "honest, upright and conscientious will never be denied," the *Messenger* asserted on March 28. "If he erred it was in placing too much confidence in convicts and subordinate officers who were unworthy."

THE FIRST PROFESSIONAL penologist to head the Minnesota prison was Albert Garvin, who assumed the post of warden in February 1891. He had received his training at the Illinois State Prison in Joliet. There was talk that Garvin, friendly to the contracting company, was chosen through its influence; whatever the reason, during his short stay at Stillwater he brought discipline back into prison life. This warden, whom the prisoners themselves called

Albert Garvin was trained at the Illinois State Prison in Joliet before he became warden at Stillwater from January 1891 to June 1892. A strict disciplinarian, he established the grading system but left the prison to become the St. Paul chief of police.

"fearlessly progressive," also did most of the spadework in establishing a grading system and a prison school. Garvin, however, remained at Stillwater only a year and a half before he moved on to become St. Paul's chief of police.[37]

His work was ably continued in June 1892 by Henry Wolfer, who was picked to head the state institution on his record of twenty years' experience as another Joliet-trained penologist. Wolfer soon established himself as the most important agent for reform in the prison's history. Almost immediately upon his arrival, he convinced Governor William R. Merriam to grant conditional pardons to deserving men. Ordered on an experimental basis in 1892, pardons were authorized by state laws the following year. The power of granting them rested solely in the hands of the governor until 1897, when a board, consisting of the governor, the chief justice of the supreme court, and the attorney general, was given the responsibility. Wolfer also created new hospital quarters on the second floor of the solitary building, allowing patients larger cells as well as separating the sick from the general population. He had workers excavate the lightless bottom floor of the twine shop and install windows. Most importantly, Garvin's plan for a grading system for prisoners was fully instituted under Wolfer in 1893, and new privileges were put in place for those who demonstrated good behavior. A new dining room with a better and varied menu was built to "stimulate ambition to gain and keep places in the first grade." That same year, he formally established the prison school under Carlton C. Aylard, principal of the Stillwater High School, for prisoners with demonstrated records of good behavior.[38]

While Wolfer was anxious to provide all inmates with the opportunity to reform, he did not romanticize them by any means. As one of his first acts as warden, he added the Bertillon method to the disciplinary department. A forerunner to the fingerprint system, the Bertillon method recorded vital measurements of an inmate's face, hands, and feet, along with full-face and profile photographs to aid in identification. Wolfer saw this as an essential partner to the parole system. "It leaves in the hands of the officials a description so perfect of the released convict," he wrote, "that should he violate the conditions of his parole, or again lapse into a life of crime, the problem of his speedy apprehension is reduced almost to a certainty." In 1894, to further assure that paroled inmates didn't stray, Wolfer created the position

Henry Wolfer, Stillwater's most significant reformer, served as warden from June 1892 to November 1914, except for a year-long departure to pursue a business opportunity. He oversaw the construction of the new prison at Bayport.

of state agent, now called a parole officer, to lead parolees "into safe surroundings and employment, with continued friendly oversight and encouragement." He also completed the work on the north wall of the prison and closed up the windows and old gateways that faced out onto Main Street to limit the possibility of escape. Wolfer made clear: he wanted those who behaved well and earned parole to succeed outside the prison, but those with time to serve or unwilling to reform he wanted safely confined within the prison walls.[39]

Wolfer had been at Stillwater only two years when the Minnesota Thresher Company failed, throwing 350 inmates out of work. To give them

Stillwater prison, about 1895

employment, Wolfer diversified the kinds of goods the prison produced, expanding from twine, foundry work, and woodworking into areas as broad-ranging as the manufacture of high school scientific apparati and men's shoes. Such work he brought in on a "piece price" system. Under this agreement, the state (and the inmate in return) would be paid according to output; this was yet another example of Wolfer's belief in a reward system.[40]

The damp, poorly ventilated, often roach-infested buildings were inadequate, however, for such new kinds of work. In 1898, Wolfer leveled the old building where the Minnesota Thresher Company had been housed, because it was unfit for workers. "Bed bugs are so numerous," com-

plained inmate Samuel A. Phillips, "they drive the average prisoner wild with pain and annoyance. The air is foul. The stench is almost intolerable." Wolfer urged the state to allocate funds for a fireproof cell house and modern factory facilities. His requests went unheeded.[41]

At a special meeting of the board of prison managers in November 1899, Wolfer resigned as warden. His experience running the twine shops at Stillwater made him an attractive candidate to the Northwestern Grass Twine Company, who hired Wolfer as general manager of their three plants in St. Paul, West Superior, and Oshkosh. He was quick to point out to the board that his salary would be "three times as great as that of warden" and he moved his family to St. Paul. In his place, the board named General Charles McCormick Reeve.[42]

Reeve appears to have been primarily a political appointment. Though he had seven years of experience running a flour mill in Minneapolis, he was best known to most Minnesotans as the colonel of the 13th Minnesota in the

Charles McCormick Reeve served as warden during Henry Wolfer's absence from December 1899 to March 1901.

Spanish-American War who had been brevetted to brigadier general for "gallant and meritorious conduct in the battle of Manila." Ironically, upon his appointment, Reeve was instructed: "Political partisan interest must never be consulted. Competent and efficient officers shall not be removed to give place to those not known to have superior qualifications and experience." True to his commitment, Reeve did not make any personnel changes during his brief tenure.[43]

The reasons are unclear but in February 1902, Warden Reeve resigned his post and the board of pardoners reinstated the "familiar face" of Henry Wolfer. After twenty-five years devoted to prison work, perhaps he found the business world foreign and frustrating. Perhaps the political climate had changed just enough that Wolfer saw the opportunity to realize his ultimate goal for the state prison. Less than six months after he was renamed warden, he wrote that "the increase in the criminal population of this State brings us face to face with one of two alternatives; either the speedy preparation for the building of a new Prison, or the overhauling of the old Prison." He reiterated

this dilemma in 1904, and the Minnesota legislature finally recognized the need.[44]

After it provided in 1905 and 1909 for new buildings to be constructed a few miles south of Stillwater, the end of the antiquated institution in Battle Hollow approached rapidly. Extensive new structures on the St. Croix River at Bayport replaced the crowded quarters that were "not fit to keep hogs in, let alone human beings." By 1914 the final contract with a shoe company expired, and only then were the last of the inmates removed to the model new prison built under Warden Wolfer's supervision.[45]

Wolfer often strolled the grounds of the prison with his St. Bernard.

In October 1914, with his highest goal realized, Wolfer retired from his position as warden and moved his family to Long Beach, California. The new facility at Bayport continued Minnesota's reputation as home to what Blake McKelvey, in his book *American Prisons*, called "the best state prison in the country throughout the era."[46]

FRESH FISH

Through the Gates

George L. Bartlett, #4342

Convicted of second-degree forgery, George L. Bartlett was sentenced to an indeterminate period of one to ten years. "Whether I am innocent or guilty," he wrote, "does not in any way concern this story." Instead, he straightforwardly described his terrifying arrival at Stillwater.

At 4 o'clock, on a cloudy fall afternoon in 1913, I entered the gates of the Old Prison at Stillwater, Minnesota.

My first impression of the officer who met me "between the gates" was, that I had never in all my life seen a rougher, gruffer man, a stronger man physically and mentally, or with such power in every line of his makeup.

"Come on," he roared at me. I was scared through and through, and perfectly "tame" from that time on.

As we passed through the Officers' Barber Shop and Kitchen, I expected every moment to get a rap on the head from the big red cane that Deputy Warden Sullivan was swinging close behind me. "Hey, Vollmer, fix this fresh fish up," he called to the Captain of the Cell House.

I (the "fresh fish" just caught) was quickly stripped of my clothing, carefully searched and examined and shoved into an old barber chair where a convict barber (or boiler maker) clipped and pulled all the hair from my head. I was then in the corridor of the Cell House.

In an old blanket bath robe and cloth slippers I

FACING PAGE: Deputy Warden Jonas Backland and two unidentified inmates at the front gate of the prison, 1907. RIGHT: Lock to the front gate

was hustled across a small yard into the Bath House, where I had a shower bath and was given underclothing and socks. The shirt and drawers were of coarse, heavy yellow-white cotton flannel, and the socks of rough gray knitted yarn, made in the prison. Upstairs above the Bath

Commitment Form for George L. Bartlett, 1913

House, in the Store Room, I was given a coat, cap and trousers of coarse, brown canvas, and pair of heavy, square toed, black, working boots.

Everything was too small for me except my hat and shoes, which were three sizes too large, and it was all I could do to walk down stairs. I went into the Cell House again, where I had undressed. Some one yelled, "Take off your hat," and I wished that they had said "shoes" instead.

The Cell House Captain gave me a receipt for my keys, cuff buttons, and little things I had in my pockets, and asked if I wanted my clothes destroyed or put in storage until I was released. I said I wanted them saved, and a few days later was given a receipt for my suit, hat, belt, underclothing and shirt. My pipes, tobacco and handkerchiefs had been tied up in a red bandanna and labeled with my name and number by the Cell House Captain and placed in his desk. I was next commanded to face the wall with folded arms. I obeyed, and stood in that position for ten minutes.

"Come on," said the Guard, and I followed him up a narrow iron stairway to the first gallery of the Cell House to a "receiving cell" where new men were placed. I found myself in a solid stone "room" with white-washed walls and sheet steel

floor, about seven feet long, five feet wide and eight feet high, and a steel barred door. An iron cot, three feet wide, hinged to the wall, a wooden chair and a small shelf on the back wall, constituted the furniture.

A tin basin, brown water crock, two tin cups, a spoon, small looking glass, library catalog, rule book, pen and ink, night bucket (set in a niche in the wall), iron cuspidor, mattress, two sheets, two blankets and a pillow on the cot, constituted the

CELL SIZE
from the *Handbook of the Minnesota State Prison*, 1909
The average size of each cell is 5x7x8—a total of 270 cubic feet. Some are a trifle larger. Medical authorities who have given the subject careful study and made exhaustive investigations are agreed that no one should be confined permanently in a room of less than 600 cubic feet. However, with good, pure air in abundance and perfect ventilation the space could with safety be cut to 400 cubic feet without endangering the health or energy of the occupant. The cells in the old prison are not only small and poorly ventilated but they do not contain the necessary toilet requisites, including running water to promote or at least conserve the health of the occupants.

Interior, men's cell, from a postcard about 1909

Deputy Warden Sullivan, 1913

entire equipment of my future home. I examined the mattress and pillow, which were of straw or corn husks, and then looked at the steel floor, wondering on which I could sleep more comfortably.

The one shadeless electric light bulb, strung on a long wire above my head, seemed of a thousand candle power, throwing a maddening glare from the dead white walls. I was afraid to turn it out or move it,—afraid to undress and try to sleep—afraid to keep my clothes on and stay awake. I wondered what they would do with me and to me.

As my thoughts ran riot on these and many other things I was brought to my senses by a loud report, close to my ear. I jumped up, but it was nothing more deadly than a library book thrown into my cell on the steel flooring. I noticed then how plainly I could hear the sound of stockinged feet on the floor, while even my own breathing seemed to echo through the small cell.

"Put out your cup for tea," a gruff voice commanded, when a tin of oatmeal with two slices of bread was shoved through the door at me. There was no sugar, or milk on the oatmeal, but it was hot and tasted good, but there was not enough of it. The bread was as good as any I had ever eaten, and fresh and sweet, and the tea was hot.

Suddenly a banging and a roar that was all but deafening, from the steel galleries about me, interrupted my supper. It was the men coming in from their day's work in the shops, walking to their cells, over the gallery floors and stairs. Then came again that dead, ghastly silence.

Occasionally a guard walked past my door, looked in, and passed on without a word. A big, pleasant-faced officer stopped.

"Watch'yer in here for?" he asked me.

"Forgery," I answered.

"That's ten years, but maybe they won't keep you but four or five," and he passed on.

That was Dan McKenzie, one of the best hearted, squarest officers in the prison, and what he said, I learned later, was intended to cheer me up.

Two men stopped at my door, one was Deputy Warden Sullivan, and the other, a man in citizen's clothes. "This is the man, Professor," said Sullivan. Then Professor Holland, the prison school principal, asked me what college I had attended, and a few questions concerning my studies. They went away, talking quietly together. What was I the man for? What other crime did they intend to fasten upon me?

The light went out at 9 o'clock, and after I had done some hard thinking, on that equally hard mattress, I fell asleep.

The First Day

George L. Bartlett, #4342

No sooner had Bartlett found some comfort in sleep than he was rudely awakened and forced to face his first full day in confinement. He was processed, assigned his inmate number, and introduced to his new daily routine.

The banging of a big gong in the corridor below, awoke me. I did not know what time it was, for it was still dark, and I hardly realized where I was. I dressed hurriedly, washed my face and hands in the little tin basin, with water from the crock, and sat down and waited.

Breakfast was shoved under my door, a plate of hash swimming in a thick syrup, two slices of bread and a large cup of "tea." I found they called it coffee in the morning, and I often later heard it called worse names than that. It was all alike, tasteless, colored water.

The clock over the Cell House Captain's desk said a little past seven when I was unlocked and told to come down. After a few moments waiting with folded arms, facing the wall in the corridor below, I was taken to the door of the Cell House and started up the "main street" of the prison yard, alone. I was given the red bandanna, and told to give it to the officer in charge of the Hospital at the head of the street.

On my left was the Cell House and Library; on my right the shops, already busy with the hum of machinery. I could see the men moving about at their work, and wondered in which I should find my job.

A walk of about three hundred yards brought me to the door of the Deputy's Office and Hospital, where an officer awaited me. Just before I got there I saw him wave his hand. Glancing over my shoulder I saw the officer who had started me out, wave his hand in reply, and go back into the Cell House.

I understood then that they did not intend to lose sight of me for a moment, but at the same time wondered where they might expect me to run, if I did run. I could see nothing but stone walls and big buildings on every side, with armed guards pacing the walls.

The officer took my little red bundle and directed me to a room on the left where my fingerprint records were made. A statement was given me to sign, authorizing the Warden or his agent, to open and inspect all letters, parcels, express and mail matter that came directed to me. I asked the officer what would happen if I did not sign it. "Nothing," he said, "only you won't get any mail." I signed, and attested it with a print of my right forefinger.

I was shown a cell, where Captain French, the officer, explained in detail how I was to care for my cell, with a general idea of the rules: I must polish my steel floor every morning with emery paper and sand; clean my cuspidor thoroughly daily; keep my cups, spoon and basin bright and free from rust; make my bed by tucking the blankets in all around and folding one sheet across the top on the outside, leaving the other on the bed under the blankets; not talk or communicate in any manner with other prisoners; always salute an officer when passing, and fold my arms and keep my eyes straight to the front when standing still at any time. My number was "4342," by which, I was told, I would be known from then on.

Captain French then took me to the Deputy's office where I was ordered to "sit down," and Deputy Warden Sullivan, at his desk in front of me, asked my name. I told him and he roared out:

"No, not that one, your RIGHT name."

An inmate clerk was making notes of my answers. I told the Deputy that I had no other name and never had, and he informed me in very plain language that I was lying, and passed on to the general examination. Where had I ever "done time" before? I told him this was the first time I had ever been in prison and he again told me I was lying, and that it would be best for me to tell the truth, as he was going to find out all about me anyway, and it would only go harder with me in the end, if he caught me in a lie.

After he had managed to totally subdue and scare me half to death, he went on with other questions as to my birthplace, names and addresses of my parents, whether either had ever been in

prison, or insane, did I or they use tobacco, drugs, or intoxicating liquors, and a short statement of the crime for which I was convicted.

Every now and then he would roar "WHAT?" in my face, not seeming to be impressed at any time with the truth of my statements.

The Deputy asked me what work I was able to do. I said I understood something of general office work and correspondence, and was a college graduate. "Here's the man, Doc," he said, calling to the prison physician, as he shoved me up the stairs ahead of him. "Sit down there," the

"Main Street" of Stillwater Prison yard, 1905

doctor said, handing me a pen. "Write this: 'On Mount Maria's pointed tops,'" he quoted. I wrote it and he smiled and said to the Deputy: "He's all right, I guess, give him a trial."

We went downstairs to the office again and the Deputy called in his clerk, the one who had taken notes at my examination. "Here's a man that's been here twenty-one years," the Deputy said. "He's my clerk and during all this time he's never been in any trouble. He has the best job in the place. He's going out soon and if you will show me that you are on the level and give me a square deal, I'll give you one and you can have his job. If you can do the work, know enough to keep your mouth shut, obey all the rules and take orders from no one but me, you will get along all right. Get out'er here." That was my appointment as confidential clerk to Deputy Warden J. J. Sullivan, in which position I remained until released.

In the room where I had been fingerprinted, the clerk showed me where to hang my coat, telling me we could talk quietly. He introduced himself as Murphy, and after telling me something of himself, started in to "wise me up to things," as he expressed it.

Murphy was convicted at the age of 30 for murder, and sentenced to life imprisonment. He had been in the prison 21 years, and aged only in years as the outside world had stood still for him. When first committed, he was practically uneducated. When I met him, he was a good general office man, fast and accurate in shorthand and wrote a splendid long hand, having educated himself under such adverse circumstances.

Mug shot of John Murphy, as he appeared shortly after he was committed to Stillwater in the 1880s

How he had stood up under the grind was hard to understand. He was sound mentally and physically. During his entire "time" he had never been in any serious trouble, and was liked and respected by officers and inmates.

In September, 1914, shortly after I was released, the Supreme Court of Minnesota settled in Murphy's favor a question of good time allowance, after his life sentence had been commuted to 30 years by the Pardon Board, which gave him his liberty. He is now employed by a St. Paul shoe company, a respected, well-behaved citizen, earning a good living and of some use to society.

After explaining some of the more important things that I must and must not do, Murphy told me I was working for the best man in the institution (Sullivan), and that I would soon know and understand him better. What I had written in the doctor's office upstairs was given me to see if I knew enough to put the apostrophe in "Maria's." Luckily, I did, which, as I was told later by the doctor, got me the job as Deputy's clerk. The Deputy had been looking for a man to take Murphy's place, who expected to be released soon, and I appeared on the scene at the opportune moment.

Most statements new prisoners made were discredited. The Deputy had called me a liar on general principles when I told him my name, and that I had never been in prison before. When I had occasion to act as examining clerk for other "fresh fish" I learned that each was handled the same as I had been, and in many cases when a man was not telling the truth, the "bluff" worked. If a man was truthful these methods did no harm,

but where he was of vicious temperament and a "bad actor," the manner and methods of the Deputy were very much inclined to knock any "bad" ideas out of his head before they became deeply rooted.

Besides his good advice and information, Murphy did much to lighten the burden of my first two weeks of horror. Shoes, socks and toilet articles, other than furnished by the state could be purchased once each month, and then only when a man had money. I had brought no money with me, not knowing that I could use it. Murphy gave me a pair of light weight black socks and a tooth brush, and had my tan shoes, which I had worn when arriving, blackened, so I could wear them instead of the heavy working boots.

No toothbrushes were furnished by the state and only black shoes allowed to be worn. What I would have done without this help from Murphy would have been the same that other men did when they first arrived—do without. No bartering, selling or exchanging of articles was permitted, and had I not been so fortunately situated in the Deputy's office, I would not have had these little comforts.

A place was made for me at a small table and I started on my first work as the Deputy's clerk.

Register No. *4342*	Name *George L. Bartlett*	✓ **487**
	Alias	

16765-12 BROWN TREACY & SPERRY CO. MFG. STRS. ST. PAUL AND MINNEAPOLIS

Term Expires		
Oct 14 1920.	**Court Record**	County
County	*Hennepin*	
	Crime *Forgery - second degree*	
Discharged	Term *Ind - (0-10) commuted by Bd of Pardons 1/27/14 to 1 year.*	
	Received *October 27th, 1913.*	
	Deposit	
	Terms served in other prisons	

PERSONAL RECORD

Nationality *Maryland*   Age *31* years, Color *White*   Religion *Episcopalian*
Occupation *Salesman Clerk*   Height *6* feet *7/8* inches. Weight   pounds. Build *m musc.*
Complexion *Fair*   Hair *m ch* Beard   Eyes *Ag Ble*
Grade of Education *College*   Habits *moderate*   Married or Single? *Married*
Nativity of Parents—Father *Penna.*   Mother *Maryland.*

DISCHARGE AND PAROLE RECORD

Paroled
Discharged *Aug 26 - 1914.*

RECORD OF SOLITARY CONFINEMENT AND GOOD TIME LOST

DAYS LOST	DATE	DAYS LOST
	1913 - 10 - 27	
	10 -	
	1914 - 8 - 26	

George L. Bartlett's entry in the convict record for 1913

To my surprise it was the making out of my own papers and records. I entered my name and number in the record book, where shop cell locations of every man in the institution were kept. A form was filled in from the information given the Deputy when I was examined and sent to the general office, where it was filed with the commitment papers and letters pertaining to my case. An index card was made out bearing my completed record and filed with the cards of all the other men in the institution.

The next day one full-face and one profile picture were made of me in the photograph gallery. My Bertillon measurements were taken later by the Deputy, and with an examination by the doctor as to my physical condition, my records were complete, and I was a "full-fledged" member of the "inside world of the Silent City."

All these entries and records, even to my own Bertillon measurements, I made myself in my own handwriting. I was told by Sullivan, shortly before I was released, that I was probably the only man in the 64 years of the existence of the prison who had entered his own records in his own handwriting.

THE CONVICT RECORD

The convict record at the old State Prison contained all basic information on each inmate, including their court records, personal information, parole record, and comments on good time lost and time spent in solitary confinement. Such information played a crucial role in pardon and parole board hearings. Even after all the inmates in each register had been released or died, the state kept these log books for reference, and they eventually became part of the state archives.

The convict record book for 1912–1914

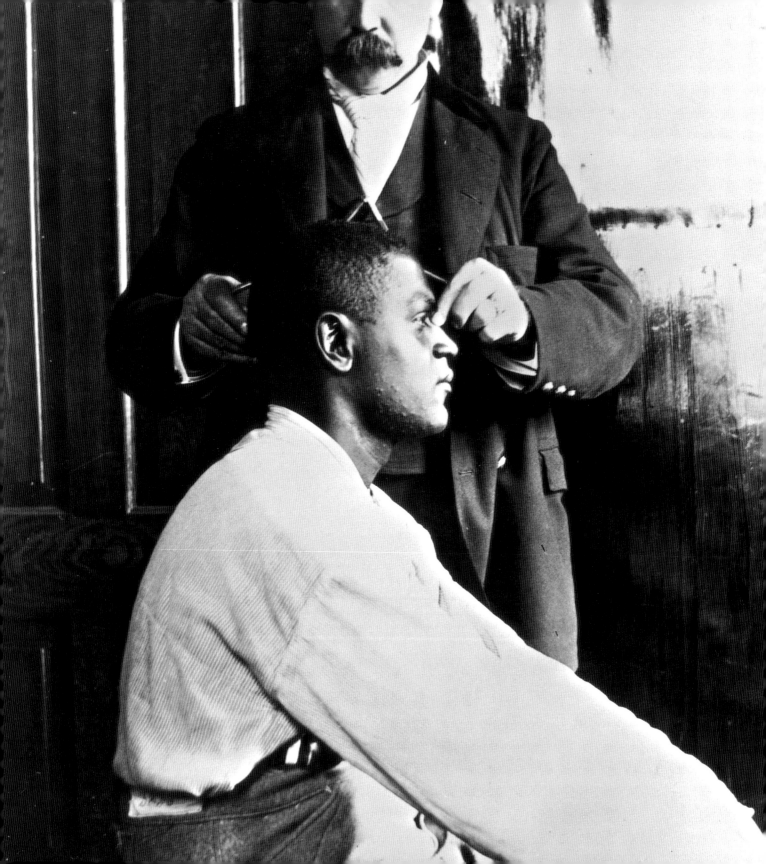

The Bertillon Method

In the days before fingerprinting, criminologists and penalogists used a variety of methods to positively identify suspects and record convicts in case of escape. The most widely accepted was the Bertillon Method, developed by the French anthropologist Dr. Alphonse Bertillon and first implemented in the United States in 1887. In his book Convict Life at the Minnesota State Prison, *W. C. Heilbron explained the technique.*

The system embraces three distinct parts: First, the measurements of certain unchangeable "bony lengths" of the body; second, a careful description of the features of the face; third, a careful localization of all scars and marks on the body. While the face may change, be even mutilated beyond recognition; while the scars and other marks may be removed, the "bony lengths" of the body remain unchangeable in adults. The parts measured of the bony lengths of the body are the length and width of the head, the cheek width, length of foot, the middle and little finger and the cubit, i. e., from the elbow to the tip of the little finger; the height standing, the height seated, the reach of outstretched arms, right ear length (which most authorities assert remains the same throughout life), the median line in front from the fork or hollow below the "Adam's apple" down, and, in the rear, the spinal column from the seventh vertebra to the base of the spine, are the anatomical or "guiding points" from which all descriptions of the body are recorded; in the finger, the joints and flanges,— the flanges being the portions of the fingers between the joints.

The technical terms used in the description of scars or marks are strictly medical. For instance, if a man has a scar on his left breast it is described as rectilinal, vertical, horizontal, inal,—such a distance from the median, and to the right, left, above or below the nipple. Scars on the fingers are described in the same terms, indicating the flange and joint, and so on through all parts of the body,—every mark, cut or bruise being measured in front, from the median line, and in the rear, from the spinal column.

With reference to the ears, there are certain external features by which scientists assert criminals may be instantly detected. Have you a criminal ear? Dr. D. S. Lamb, at one time curator in charge of the Army Medical Museum, says there

LEFT MIDDLE FINGER MEASUREMENT.

HEAD LENGTH MEASUREMENTS.

RIGHT EAR AND TRUNK MEASUREMENTS.

MEASUREMENTS OF OUTSTRETCHED ARMS & LEFT FOOT.

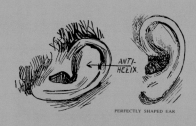

ANTI-HELIX

PERFECTLY SHAPED EAR

How to take Bertillon measurements, from Heilbron's *Convict Life at the Minnesota State Prison*

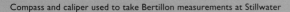

is such a thing as a "criminal ear." Anthropologists have been giving a great deal of study to the matter of late, and their data points to the conclusion that the term "ear-mark" is something more than a mere figure of speech. No one has two ears just alike; all ears are faulty in one way or another, that is, as to size, shape or position, and these organs do not stop growing when the body pauses in its development. At all events, chronic malefactors are apt to be disfigured by certain malformations of that organ. It has been proven that abnormalities in the ear structure are characteristic features of degenerates. Such abnormalities are commonly found in idiots, imbeciles and epileptics, and the prisons contain quite a number of inmates with such ears.

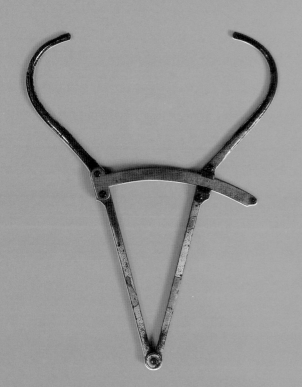

Compass and caliper used to take Bertillon measurements at Stillwater

Mug Shots

Despite the exactness of his measurements and the extremely remote possibility of two people with identical descriptions, Bertillon introduced the use of photography to his method. He recommended that each suspect be photographed full face and in profile. The profile portrait was especially important to Bertillon, because it provided a detailed look at the ear. He also required photographs of all suspects to be taken from the same distance, in order to establish scale.

By the time officials at the Minnesota State Prison began using the system in the 1890s, "Bertillon photographs," now known as mug shots, were a standard feature and copies of mug shots were sent to a central system in New York. Within a matter of weeks, prisoners who had entered the

LEFT: Charles Hastings, #4606, sentenced in March 1897 to five years for first-degree grand larceny, in an uncropped mug shot. TOP: The camera used by John Runk to take mug shots

prison under a false name or claimed to have no prior record could be matched against their central file. Photographs of escapees could also be distributed to local authorities and posted in town post offices to effect their capture.

No one knows for sure who the first photographer or photographers were at Stillwater. John M. Kuhn and his brother Louis, both prominent local photographers in the 1890s, took official photographs of the guards and wardens, so they are the most likely candidates. They were also mentors to John Runk, the photographer who took over the responsibility around the turn of the century.

John Runk's self-portrait, taken in the prison about 1903

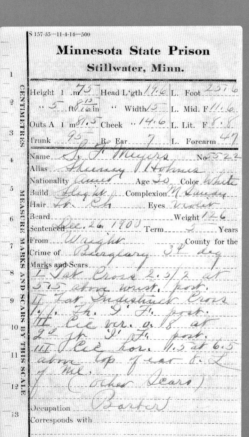

Minnesota State Prison
Stillwater, Minn.

S 157-35—11-4-14—500

Height 1 m 75	Head L'gth 19.6	L. Foot 25.6
" 5 ft 9½ in	" Width 15	L. Mid. F 11.6
Outs A 1 m 81.5	Cheek " 14.6	L. Lit. F 8.8
Trunk 95	R. Ear 7	L. Forearm 47

Name G. F. Meyers No. 5522
Alias Shumey Holmes
Nationality Amer Age 30 Color White
Build Slight Complexion M. Sandy
Hair Lr. Ch Eyes Violet
Beard Weight 126
Sentenced Dec. 26, 1900 Term 5 Years
From Wright County for the
Crime of Burglary 3d deg
Marks and Scars
I. Tat Cross 2.3/2 at 5.5 above wrist post.
II. Tat Indistinct Cross 1.4 Th. D'F. post.
III. Cic ver. 0.8 at 2d jt. D'F. post.
IV. Cic hor. 1.5 at 6.5 above top of ear 8. L of M. (other Scars)

Occupation Barber
Corresponds with

MINNESOTA STATE PRISON
STILLWATER, MINN.

Height 1 m 673	Head L'gth 18.8	L. Foot 23.4
" 5 5⅛ in	" Width 15.4	L. Mid. F 11.7
Outs A 1 m 75	Cheek " 13.8	L. Lit. F 9.
Trunk 98.2	R. Ear 6.3	L. Forearm 45.8

Name Chas H. Howard No. 1020
Alias Cheerful Charley
Nationality American Age 27 Color White
Build Slight Erect Complexion Florid
Hair Dk. ch Eyes Lt. ch
Beard Weight 140
Sentenced Apr 1903 Term 3⅓ Years
From St. Louis County for the
Crime of Forgery 2d
Marks and Scars
I. sc. irr 1.5 x 0.2 @ 2d jt. L Fin
I. " " 1 x 0.2 th L Fin.
I. " 0.7 x 0.7 @ 2d jt S F
I. " hor. 2 x 0.5 @ 18 ↗ int jt 4
5 ↙ elbow jt in

Occupation Clerk
Corresponds with

F. P. Class

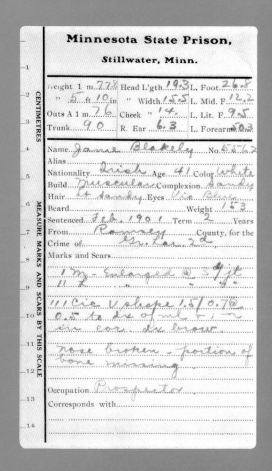

Minnesota State Prison,
Stillwater, Minn.

Height 1 m. 80.7	Head L'gth 20.2	L. Foot 27.2
" 5 ft 11½ in	" Width 14.7	L. Mid. F 12.4
Outs A 1 m. 84	Cheek " 14.4	L. Lit. F 9.3
Trunk 95.8	R. Ear 6.4	L. Forearm 49.8

Name....John W. Kelly....No....919
Alias....
Nationality....Irish....Age....45....Color....White
Build....St. Erect....Complexion....Florid
Hair....Dk. Sandy....Eyes....pale blue
Beard....Weight....184
Sentenced..Dec., 1902....Term....20....Year
From....Clay....County, for th
Crime of....Sodomy.

Marks and Scars.
I Tat.—Irr. 2x1 at 5 above wrist joint in.
I Tat.—Ballet Girl 10.5x4 at 6 above wrist joint. 3
   under elbow joint in.
II—Scar irr. 2.5x0.2 at outer corner of left brow.
II—Scar irr. 1x0.2 at right cheek, 5 from coroner of
   mouth.
II—Scar rec. 1.5x0.1 at 5.5 right ml. 5 abovr outer
   coroner right brow.

Occupation....
Corresponds with....

Minnesota State Prison,
Stillwater, Minn.

Height 1 m. 7.78	Head L'gth 19.3	L. Foot 26.8
" 5 ft 10 in	" Width 15.5	L. Mid. F 12.2
Outs A 1 m. 76	Cheek " 14.5	L. Lit. F 9.5
Trunk 90	R. Ear 6.3	L. Forearm 50.3

Name....James Blakely....No....5562
Alias....
Nationality....Irish....Age....41....Color....White
Build....Muscular....Complexion....Sandy
Hair....Lt. Sandy....Eyes....Vio Blue
Beard....Weight....153
Sentenced..Feb. 1901....Term....2....Years
From....Ramsey....County, for the
Crime of....Gr. Lar. 2d

Marks and Scars....

1 M—Enlarged @ 3 ft.
11 L " " " "
111 Cic V shape 1.5/0.7 @
0.5 to dr of ml 1 in
   in ear ... dr. brow
nose broken - portion of
bone missing

Occupation....Prospector
Corresponds with....

The Grading System

Beginning in the 1890s, prisoners were divided according to a "Merit and Grade System," which was designed to allow each inmate to "work out his own salvation." Thus, behavior became the standard by which prisoners were afforded privileges and by which recommendations to the pardons board for diminution of sentences were determined. The Handbook of the Minnesota State Prison (1903) explained the system in detail.

Prisoners are separated into three grades—first, second and third. The first is the highest. Its garb consists of a neat grey suit and cap. First grade prisoners are entitled to write one letter each week, to draw a ration (four ounces)

LEFT: Unidentified inmate in the checked uniform of the second grade. This was one of three photographs used in a postcard showing all three grades (above).

of tobacco weekly, and to receive visitors once in four weeks. They have a dining room to themselves and are served with a greater variety of food than are the prisoners in the other grades. They have also such other privileges granted them from time to time as their general conduct warrants.

Prisoners in the second grade are clothed in a black and grey check suit and cap. They are permitted to write one letter a fortnight, to draw a ration of tobacco weekly and to see visitors once a month. They also have a dining-room of their own, but the food served therein is not as varied as that served to first grade men. The latter, for example, are served with butter and other relishes at stated intervals, but such things are not part of the diet of the second grade prisoners.

Inmates in the third grade wear black and white striped suits. They are denied tobacco, writing and visiting privileges and their meals are served in their cells, which are located in one portion of the cellhouse. In none of the grades are prisoners required to march with the "lock-step," and excepting those in the third grade, all are permitted to wear their hair long enough to comb during good behavior.

Upon entering the institution, the prisoner is assigned to the second grade. If he earns fifty out of a possible fifty-four credit marks in the course of six months, he is advanced to the first grade; but if he fails to earn the required number of merit marks he must remain in the second grade until he does earn them in six consecutive months, provided his conduct is such that he does not descend to the third grade. A prisoner is degraded if he loses more than two credit marks within a month, and in case this occurs he must keep an absolutely clear record for one month in order to regain the next higher grade.

Writing, visiting and smoking privileges are manifested by small tickets which are given the prisoner on his entrance to the institution, and which must be produced when he desires to make use of them. The loss of these tickets, through a violation of the rules, entails the loss of the privileges they represent.

BEING MUGGED
Samuel A. Phillips, #2479

When a man is taken to prison, he is mugged after being close-cropped and encased in prison costume. He is an ugly, repellant-looking creature in such attire and a several days' growth of beard upon his face. These photographs are sent to a central exchange with descriptions of the prisoners and the originals are looked upon as suspects all over the country. If anything goes wrong, nip one of them. His power of resistance is so weak he cannot put up a fight and perhaps upon the slightest pretext or excuse is sent to prison again.

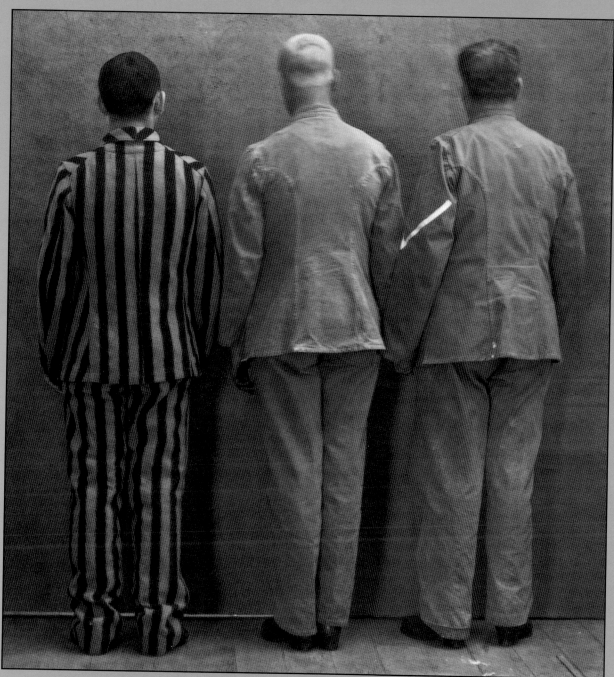

About 1910 the prison garb was changed to striped uniforms for the third grade, gray uniforms for the second grade, and gray uniforms with a stripe on the sleeve for the first grade.

LIFE ON
the INSIDE

To Prison for Life

Cole Younger, #700

Thomas Coleman ("Cole") Younger was one of the nineteenth century's most celebrated desperadoes, robbing banks and trains with Jesse and Frank James and with his brothers, Bob and Jim Younger. An ill-fated attempt on the Northfield Bank in September 1876, however, landed the Younger brothers in Stillwater prison for the next twenty-five years.

Four indictments were found against us. One charged us with being accessory to the murder of Cashier Heywood, another with assaulting Bunker with intent to do great bodily harm, and the third with robbing the First National Bank of Northfield. The fourth charged me as principal and my brothers as accessories

The cell house captain at his desk with Deputy Warden Jonas Backland in the interior cell house about 1905. Note the signal bell above the captain's desk.

with the murder of Gustavson. Two witnesses had testified before the grand jury identifying me as the man who fired the shot that hit him, although I know I did not, because I fired no shot in that part of town.

Although no one of us had fired the shot that killed either Heywood or Gustavson, our attorneys, Thomas Rutledge of Madelia and Bachelder and Buckham of Faribault, asked, when we were arraigned, Nov. 9, that we be given two days in which to plead.

They advised us that as accessories were equally guilty with the principals, under the law, and as by pleading guilty we could escape capital punishment, we should plead guilty. There was little doubt, under the circumstances, of our conviction, and under the law as it stood then, an

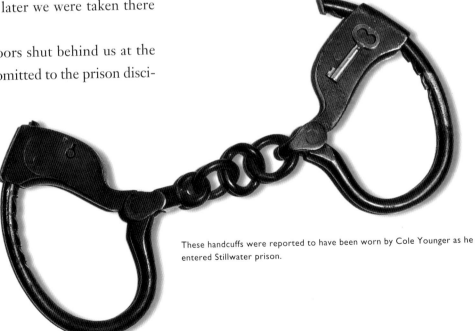

accused murderer who pleaded guilty was not subject to the death penalty. The state was new, and the law had been made to offer an inducement to murderers not to put the county to the expense of a trial.

The excitement that followed our sentence to state prison, which was popularly called "cheating the gallows," resulted in the change of the law in that respect.

The following Sunday we pleaded guilty, and Judge Lord sentenced us to imprisonment for the remainder of our lives in the state prison at Stillwater, and a few days later we were taken there by Sheriff Barton.

When the iron doors shut behind us at the Stillwater prison, I submitted to the prison discipline with the same unquestioning obedience that I had expected during my military service, and Jim and Bob, did the same.

The first three years there was a popular idea that such desperate men as the Youngers would not stay long behind prison walls, and that especial watchfulness must be exercised in our case. Accordingly the three of us were put at work making buckets and tubs, with Ben Cayou over us as a special guard, when in our dreams we had been traveling to South America on Ben Butler's money.

These handcuffs were reported to have been worn by Cole Younger as he entered Stillwater prison.

Henrietta Younger was allowed to enter Stillwater in 1889 to pose with her brothers (left to right), Jim, Bob, and Cole, when it was learned that Bob was dying of consumption. They received special permission to appear out of their prison uniforms.

The Daily Routine

Frank P. Landers, #2022

Over the years, the prison shops played host to various kinds of manufacturing, but none was more profitable or longer running than the production of binder twine.

At 6:45 the wall guards are dispatched to their respective stations, the shop guards summoned into the cell building where the deputy warden makes inspection and issues the orders of the day. The cells are quickly "unsloughed" by the guards and the assistant-deputy warden proceeds in systematic manner to dispatch the convicts to their several shops.

The men are called by a series of numeral signals corresponding to the different shops. As these signals are given each shop squad makes its ap-

pearance from the cell house, forms in line in the yard with the precision of an astronomo-electric clock, where it is passed under the inspection of the deputy warden and turned over to the guard of the shop, to which it is marched in double file. As one company moves off another makes its appearance in obedience to the signal call of the assistant deputy stationed inside the cell house. There are at present about 370 men at work daily, 320 on contract labor and 50 on State. The time occupied in dispatching averages 10 minutes.

So soon as the men have reached the shops the citizen laborers are admitted to the yard, and proceed to their shops. Work begins at 7 sharp.

At noon the men are marched to the cell house, the line breaking at the entrance, each man passing by the nearest route to his cell, where he finds his dinner awaiting him, having been placed there some three minutes previous.

At 12:45 the signal is given and the operation of the morning repeated, work beginning at 1. About 2 P.M. is the hour set apart by the warden to receive convicts who desire to petition for favors, argue their cases, and adjust any family differences which have baffled the ingenuity of the deputy warden or his assistants.

At 6 P.M. work is suspended, the men march to their cells in the same regular order already indicated, and receive their supper.

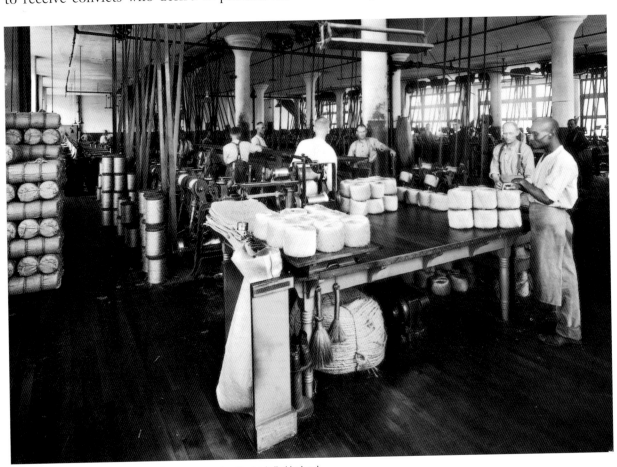

Spinning the fiber into rope and twine. Rope was wound and twine balled by hand.

Sacking and baling twine for clean, easy transport

The Women's Department

Azilda Beaudry, #1845

Azilda Beaudry was committed to the state prison on September 27, 1884, to serve a life sentence for the murder of her husband in Marshall County. When she entered Stillwater, at age twenty-seven, she left her three children in the care of relatives in Coleman, Wisconsin. In fewer than four years, all three children had died. Beaudry became a frequent contributor to the Prison Mirror *almost immediately after it was founded in August 1887. Some of her articles provide a partial record of her sorrow.*

December 18, 1887

As I sit here to-night alone with my thoughts, I will try and tell you some of them just as they come to my mind. Here hangs before me in a lit-

The inmates of the women's department were allowed to turn their backs in order to protect their anonymity, about 1905.

tle frame the picture of two dear little children. They are mine; but where are they? Far away from me. I have not seen them for over three long years, and there is but little hope for me to see them again on this earth. I have no need to say that each look at these little pictures almost breaks my heart. Christmas is drawing near and how much will I miss them and all my friends on that day; and I know that they also will miss me, and that many tears will be shed on my account. It seems hard for me sometimes to keep up and be cheerful.

January 1888, DIED in Coleman, Wis., of diphtheria, Henry Beaudry, aged 6 years, 2 months and 18 days.

The death of a loved one is always a sad event, but when that one is in the joyous years of

innocent childhood, the grief of the mother is beyond all description. It is a grief which the mother, who stood over her child in the chill embrace of death, knows; but she may gain a morsel of consolation from that last look, and cherish the memory of the last kiss of the lips of death; but to me, confined in prison, this privilege, this natural desire in the mother's heart, is denied, and my only consolation is in hope for meeting beyond the grave. I will live with no other object than to purify my soul that I may realize this hope. But oh! how dismal to think that I must live in the narrow confines of a cell. Is it possible for one to commit a crime so great that no amount of suffering will pay the penalty? Certainly if mental pain can pay the debt, the death of my three children since I have been confined here has been enough to entitle me to forgiveness.

Beaudry's pleas for forgiveness apparently did not go unheard. On April 4, 1891, she was granted a pardon by Governor Merriam. The fifty cents she had in her pocket when she arrived at the prison were returned to her, and she was released.

The number assigned this rare mug shot of a woman, #3504, corresponds to the record for Ella Demeules, alias Ella Johnson, sentenced on December 3, 1892, to sixteen months for "keeping a house of ill fame." Ella is listed, however, as having a "fair complexion."

NELLIE SULLIVAN, PRISON PROSTITUTE

Nellie Sullivan, also known as Nell Stack or Nell Stoecks, was arrested on November 25, 1869, for "running a house of ill-fame." Prison records indicate that she was five feet tall with brown hair, blue eyes, and light complected but "pox marked" skin. She was only nineteen years old. The *St. Paul Dispatch* reported that she had entered in her defense that "she rents the building of a prominent merchant and church member of Minneapolis at a certain stipulated rent, and that she pays the rent by doing 'plain sewing' for the merchant."

Perhaps it was this merchant who posted Nellie's bond, because the grand jury returned an indictment, and she was released on bail pending her court date. In June 1870, the *Minneapolis Tribune* reported:

> Nellie Sullivan (alias Nell Stack) who was indicted last fall by the grand jury for keeping a house of ill-fame and arrested in St. Paul a few days ago by Deputy Sheriff Eaton, came to trial. Her case occupied the most of yesterday, and the jury returned a verdict of guilty.

Sullivan was one of scores of prostitutes working along Minneapolis's waterfront. She was hardly unusual, but with the guilty verdict she became the first woman convicted of prostitution in Hennepin County. For her crime, she received a six-month sentence at Stillwater. The June 22 issue of the *Tribune* noted that the short sentence "was at the suggestion of the jury recommending her to the clemency of the court," because Nellie "promised the court to reform."

But that didn't prove to be the case. Within months of arriving at the prison, Nellie had worked out an arrangement with Warden Webber that would allow her and her sister Patsy to have use of the hospital cells from 10 A.M. to 2 P.M. each day, where they "were permitted to make assignation with the male convicts." When Deputy Warden Davis voiced his objections to such corruption in the prison, he was summarily fired.

Outraged by Webber's audacity, Davis filed a full report of vice in the prison to the Board of Inspectors in August 1870. Nellie and Patsy were mentioned by name. The Board of Inspectors launched a full investigation, and Nellie's prison house prostitution ring was brought to an abrupt halt.

Despite the fact that the charges were upheld and Webber was dismissed by Governor Austin, no time was added to Nellie's term. She was released December 21, 1870, upon the expiration of her sentence, and there is no further record of her or her sister.

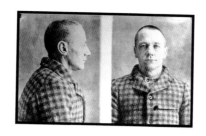

The Prison Fire

Cole Younger, #700

At 11:00 P.M. on January 8, 1884, a fire was discovered in the glazing room of the woodworking shop by the night watchman. The shops were destroyed. Unable to work, prisoners were confined to their cells until 11:15 P.M. on January 25 when, as Warden Reed recalled, "they were burned out of there." The alarm sounded due to a "dense volume of smoke" from the basement of the main building.

We had been in prison a little over seven years, when, on January 25, 1884, the main building was destroyed by fire at night. George F. Dodd was then connected with the prison, while his wife was matron. There was danger of a panic and a terrible disaster. Dodd re-

The wreckage of the prison shops the morning after the January 1884 fire (detail from a stereo view by John M. Kuhn)

leased Jim and Bob and myself. To me he gave a revolver. Jim had an axe handle and Bob a small iron bar. We stood guard over the women prisoners, marched them from the danger of the fire, and the prison authorities were kind enough

Deputy Warden Abe Hall, who refused to shackle the Youngers after the fire.

to say that had it not been for us there must have been a tremendous loss of life.

Next day Warden Reed was flooded with telegrams and newspaper sensations: "Keep close watch of the Youngers;" "Did the Youngers escape?" "Plot to free the Youngers," and that sort of thing.

This stereo view of the prison was taken only hours after the fire of 1884 (John Kuhn).

The Youngers during the Prison Fire

George P. Dodd, prison shopkeeper

I was obliged to take the female convicts from their cells and place them in a small room that could not be locked. The Youngers were passing and Cole asked if they could be of any service. I said, "Yes, Cole. Will you three boys take care of Mrs. Dodd and the women?" Cole answered: "Yes, we will, and if you ever had any confidence in us place it in us now." I told him I had the utmost confidence and I slipped a pistol to Cole as I had two. Jim, I think, had an ax handle and Bob a little pinch bar. The boys stood before the door of the little room for hours and even took the blankets they had brought with them from their cells and gave them to the women to try and keep them comfortable as it was very cold. When I could take charge of the women and the boys were relieved, Cole returned my revolver.

The warden came to his chief deputy, Abe Hall, and suggested that we be put in irons, not that he had any fear on our account, but for the effect on the public.

"I'll not put irons on 'em," replied Hall.

And that day Hall and Judge Butts took us in a sleigh down town to the county jail where we remained for three or four weeks. That was the only time we were outside the prison enclose from 1876 till 1901. I can say without fear of contradiction that had it been in our minds to do so we could have escaped from the prison that night, but we had determined to pay the penalty that had been exacted, and if we were ever to return to liberty it would be with the consent and approval of the authorities and the public.

Deaths as a Result
of the Fire
Dr. W. H. Pratt, prison physician

During and following the fire, the warden did everything in his power for the comfort of the prisoners, and no better proof of his success could be wished, than demonstrated in the fact that under his management the prisoners, without an exception, conducted themselves like men; and although everything available excepting bread was burned, the men did not lose a meal, but were provided with a warm breakfast the next morning.

Henry Lempke was suffocated during the fire. His cell door was unlocked and swung open, and he was ordered to go down. Why he did not obey is a mystery; the probabilities are that he was frightened, and being upon the upper gallery he would very soon suffocate.

Thomas Shippy was severely injured by a fall at the time of the fire, and although immediately taken to the city hospital, receiving the best of treatment and nursing, being an old man and much debilitated before the accident, he died from the effects of his injuries.

Dr. W. H. Pratt, prison physician

Though Warden Reed considered the timing of the fires "suggestive of incendiarism," no evidence of arson could be found. He wrote, "We made a very thorough investigation and can only come to one conclusion, and that is: 'Origin of the fire unknown.'"

The stock of this guard's rifle was burned away in the prison fire.

The Prison Band and Orchestra

John Carter, #1635

Music is a great civilizing influence; but the quality of prison music is not choice: it droppeth as a foretaste of purgatorial hail upon the unwilling ear. But to be pharisaical is to be beside the mark. The music is undoubtedly up to the standard of appreciation. If the only original "Southern Beauties," rag-time two-step and march, brings delight where no delight was, then on with the only original, let noise be unconfined! I owe too large a proportion of what little remains of my sanity to this same concerted conspiracy against artistic canons to condemn it utterly.

The prison band included about twenty members, who were badly handicapped by worn-out instruments, slight previous knowledge of music, and insufficient opportunities for practice and instruction. The orchestra of ten pieces was better equipped, and had attained a very fair degree of proficiency. Both band and orchestra practiced every day for an hour, but there was no opportunity for individual practice. The band played on Sundays during drill, and the orchestra furnished the music for the chapel services.

LEFT: The band on the prison's Main Street, about 1907 (John Runk). John Carter, later called the "prison poet," stands at center holding his clarinet. RIGHT: The prison orchestra, about 1910 (John Runk)

Come Up to the Library

Cole Younger, #700

The January 11, 1888, issue of the Prison Mirror *featured an editorial encouraging inmates to use the resources at the prison library in order to reform themselves. The next issue featured a response from Cole Younger, then the prison librarian.*

I noticed an article in yesterday's *Mirror* in which the writer makes suggestions as regards what we should read and what we should do while here to prepare ourselves for the fight we will have to make after we are released from here. I am pleased to admit that his advice, in my opinion, is both good and wholesome, but the writer is "off" in referring them to the library for certain books. The books mentioned are not there; neither is the writing paper of which he

The prison library, June 6, 1910 (John Runk)

speaks; the library supplies copy books for beginners only. Those who have advanced sufficiently are not allowed copy books. The number of applications to-day shows that the article was read and heeded by quite a number. I was sorry I had to refuse so many, but orders must be obeyed, you know, and experts will consequently go without copy books.

If each of us could purchase the books we require to aid us in whatever we attempted it would be money well spent. But where is the money to come from? Most of us are "dead broke" and have been since our trials; in fact, had to borrow clothes to keep from exposing ourselves at the trial. As we have not been able to save any funds since we have been boarding here, I ask again, where's the money to come from? Now, if any generous inmate has two or three thousand dollars in the bank and really wishes to aid his brother unfortunates, let him come to the front, advance us two or three dollars each and when we are discharged we will pay principal and interest.

Now, boys, if you can't do any better, come up to the library or give in your slips and you shall get standard works—history, biography, fiction, science, and religious—all good books, by eminent authors. The ablest writers the world has produced are represented in our library. The characters noble, chaste, true and good, which we all admire, are pictured in many of our volumes. The other characters, the treacherous, low, crafty, despicable, and serpent-like creatures are also here. The beautiful, attractive, and accomplished

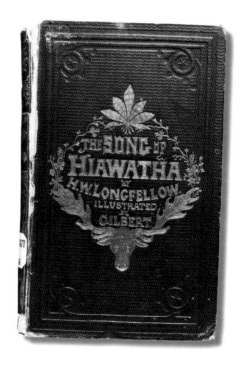

Popular titles available from the prison library at the time Younger was librarian. The library featured numerous works by Edward Eggleston, who had served briefly as the prison chaplain.

young lady with scores of admirers and everything at her command to make life a success, is not satisfied, because all the attention is not hers. Then her fickle, treacherous, damnable character shows itself. She is there also, boys.

You may ask, "What has this to do with us? Our friends are not of that sort." I hope not.

We can't all claim that we were born with silver spoons in our mouth, but we can be men, and fight the good fight with honor to ourselves, and if He makes us the father of a family we may be able to put the silver spoon in the family's mouth, and when the rewards are given for good deeds done, although the stripes are not yet erased from our back, we will get there all the same.

MEETING COLE YOUNGER

B. J., an unidentified inmate committed in August or early September 1887

B. J. tells how he was committed to the prison, shaven clean with a dull razor, denied his requests for water, and led to his cell in the prison's top gallery, "the attic, cock-loft, sky-parlor, or whatever you call it." He was mainly preoccupied with his fear of falling from the stairs to the top floor until he was locked in. Shortly thereafter, when he met the prison librarian, he found something new to worry about.

Someone came to the door and very kindly offered me a book and a newspaper. He then introduced himself—Cole Younger. Great Heavens! up on the top gallery with Cole Younger. I wished I had fallen off the gallery; that the barber had gotten a sharp razor and cut my throat, or that I had died of thirst. He looked as big as a mountain, and I felt so small that I feared he'd reach in and pull me out through the bars. It didn't take very long, however, for me to be convinced of the fact that Cole was as good as he was large, and I began to feel perfectly safe.

Sin Bad and the Greenhouse

On December 12, 1890, Charles Price was committed to Stillwater to serve a life sentence for second-degree murder after he killed a Washington County man in a "quarrel." Price quickly acquired the prison house moniker of "Sinbad the Sailor," because he was "an old salt and has sailed the seas as an Able Body and man-o'-wars-man." Price's history in the merchant marines would have been readily apparent, given the many tattoos noted on his commitment record: a ballet girl and coat of arms on his right forearm, a bracelet and anchor on his right wrist, a harp and arrow on his right hand, a crucifix and

Charles "Sin Bad" Price shows off the size of his greenhouse lemons, 1910 (John Runk). Under Sin Bad's guidance, the prison greenhouse provided a variety of fresh fruit, vegetables, and herbs for the inmates, as well as fresh flowers for the hospital rooms and staff quarters.

crown on his left forearm, and a bracelet and star on his left wrist.

He also earned a reputation for his short temper and obscene behavior. In his first six years at Stillwater, Price was sent to solitary three times:

Confined in Solitary, Aug. 29, 1892, at 5:50 A.M. for breaking cell furniture and making a disturbance in cell house. Transferred to Crank Cell August 31, 1892. 7 dys.

Oct. 9, 1893: Confined in Sol. 7:00 A.M. for Profane language to and refusing to obey officer. 7 Days and $3.50 forfeited. Released: 9 dys.

Oct. 7, 1896. Confined in the solitary for indecent motions to a lady on Second Street above the prison, the lady making complaint to wall guard Murphy. 10 days and $5.00 forfeit.

After these three early incidents, however, Price kept out of trouble, and in time he transformed his sailor nickname "Sinbad" to the more reformed "Sin Bad." His new outlook earned him a spot in charge of the new greenhouse when it was constructed along with the new hospital at the turn of the century.

With the advent of the parole system, Price's good behavior paid off even further. Samuel A. Phillips, editor of the *Prison Mirror*, took up Sinbad's case, along with John Carter's, and used his editorial space to lobby for their release. When Carter was pardoned in April 1910, Phillips wrote:

John Carter poured out the anguish of his soul in exquisite, heart-throbbing verse which attracted the attention of the world. Charles Price is of a different mould—but he is an artist, too. As a floriculturist he probably has no superior in the country. Will Justice hear his appeal?

Indeed, it did. Price was paroled on August 5, 1910, and finally discharged on October 2, 1914, having served twenty-four years.

SIN BAD

W. C. Heilbron, from *Convict Life at the Minnesota State Prison*

The greenhouse supplies flowers for decorating the lawns and parks, cut flowers for the hospital inmates, the officers' and guards' mess rooms and the room used by the members of the State Board of Control on their monthly visits to the prison. When Sin Bad becomes lonely for the wash of the sea waves his assistant throws a few buckets of water against the side of the greenhouse and he exercises his imagination for the rest.

From the *Prison Mirror*

Cal, the sorter in shop H, who is an old sea dog himself, says that the only practical experience Sin Bad and other local fisherman ever had in the whaling line was throwing the harpoon into one of these miniature whales that are habitants of Liver Brown's free lunch counter.

Sin Bad catches a nap, propped up against his wheelbarrow outside the greenhouse

The Prison Hospital

Cole Younger, #700

When Warden Wolfer came to the prison, he put Jim in charge of the mail and the library, and I was set at work in the laundry temporarily while the new hospital was being made ready. I was then made head nurse in the hospital, and remained there until the day we were paroled, Warden Reeve, who was there for two years under the administration of Gov. Lind, leaving us there.

Dr. Pratt, who was prison physician when we went to Stillwater, Dr. T. C. Clark, who was his assistant, and Dr. B. J. Merrill, who has been prison physician since, have been staunch partisans of the Younger boys in the efforts of our friends to secure our pardon. The stewards, too,

Benner, and during the Reeve regime, Smithton, with whom as head nurse I was thrown in direct contact, never had any difficulty with me, although Benner with a twinkle in his eye, would say to me:

"Cole, I believe you come and get peaches for your patients up there long after they are dead."

The invalids in that hospital always got the delicacies they wanted, subject to the physician's permission, if what they wanted was to be found anywhere in Stillwater or in St. Paul. The prison hospital building is not suitable for such use, and a new hospital is needed, but no fault can be found with the way invalid prisoners are cared for at Stillwater.

The new prison hospital, constructed in 1903

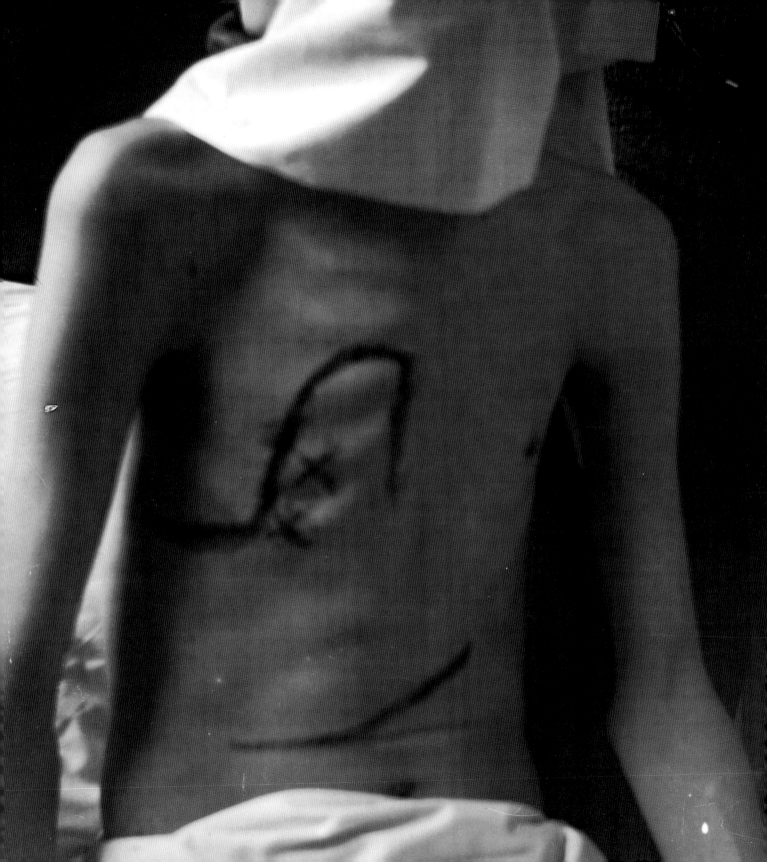

The Stabbing of Frank Lamier

Charles "Sin Bad" Price, #3210

On November 20, 1908, Frank Lamier was fatally stabbed by African American inmate James Cunningham, after Lamier called Cunningham "yellow"— a racial slur in that era. Charles Price's testimony, offered at the coroner's inquest, described how his peaceful work in the greenhouse became the catalyst for the deadly outburst.

I just came in with a box of flowers and made a motion to Frank Lamier like this. He stands near the deputy's office—there's a chair there—and I made a motion like this on the front of my body like this, with both hands. When any-

This photo, found in a private collection among glass plate negatives from the prison, is thought to be the postmortem shot of Lamier, taken for the coroner's inquest. The two stab wounds on the right side of this victim's chest seem to match Price's description of the crime.

body wants to know where the deputy is, it is the custom to rub down the front that way. It means two rows of buttons. That's the way we find out if the Deputy's about, just rub down the chest that way, and that is answered by a nod if they know where he is, and if they nod the other way then he is out. Well, I was just coming in with a box of flowers and made the sign towards the office, and Lamier nodded towards the solitary. I stood right there in the door at the entrance, and I heard somebody coming along, could hear them. There is mats on the floor, and I heard someone coming and looked up. It was Cunningham. He was coming from the bathroom or solitary department.

He said, "Give me a flower," and I nodded my head to him.

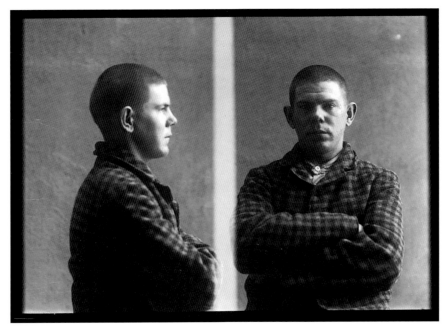

Frank Lamier, #2185, was working as a cook in Grand Rapids when he was arrested for robbery, his second offense.

Lamier said, "Don't give the big yellow stiff anything."

Cunningham then turned into the door leading to the west, facing the crank cells. Lamier slammed the door that leads in this hallway and said, "Come on, Mr. Rence, and lock this big stiff up." At the same time, Lamier pushed the door open and I heard a lick, but I didn't see what did it. I didn't know which one did it, didn't know which was struck. Then Mr. Rence went in and he said, "Come on, separate these fellows."

I stood in the door, and Mr. Rence went up to them. Lamier was down on the floor, and Cunningham was on top of him, and he said, "I don't want to hurt him, but I don't want him to hurt me either." The guard took hold of them and tried to pull them apart. He couldn't so I started to help him. I took hold of him and the guard took hold of Cunningham and told him to go to his cell.

Lamier broke away from me and got a club, and as he came back I said, "Don't do that; he is going to his cell." He gave me a push, and I sat down on the floor, and by that time he was pretty near down to where Cunningham was, and he pushed the guard aside out of his way, and the guard tried to stop him, but he struck at him. I could see Cunningham, his one foot was out, and Lamier was striking with the club at him.

I couldn't swear how many times he struck him, but he struck him more than once, that I know. That I saw. After that, I saw the knife come out, and Cunningham struck at him with it, and Lamier screamed to me, and I saw there was going to be something doing, so I took my glasses off and took out my teeth to put them out of the way. I didn't want them to get broke if there was going to be anything doing, and they was liable to, so I put them out of the way.

Lamier said, "Look at him. He has a knife as long as me arm."

He started past me and hurried up the stairs, and when he got to the top of the stairs I heard him say, "Doctor!" That was right at the top of the stairs, and just then the Deputy steps in from the solitary department and asked me what was the matter. I said, "Cunningham has cut Lamier, and he has gone upstairs," and he said, "Come on, let's get the knife." We went to the cell and got the knife. Just then the hospital nurse, Verl, came down, and he said, "We can't do nothing. Lamier is dead."

James Cunningham was serving a five-year sentence for grand larceny when he stabbed Frank Lamier. After finishing that penalty, he began serving a life sentence for Lamier's murder.

A contraband knife, more that twenty-four inches long, confiscated at the new prison a decade after the Lamier stabbing

Frank P. Landers, Stillwater's Celebrity Escapee

There were surprisingly few escapes from Stillwater. After the early territorial period, when lack of staff and inadequate walls made escapes easy and frequent, fewer than twenty men escaped from the state prison between 1858 and 1900.

On October 12, 1887, Frank P. Landers, with the assistance of Oscar J. Carlon, pulled off the most notorious escape in the early years of the state prison. Landers was serving twenty-four years for a series of forgery convictions, a term he considered excessive and unfair, and he was ill suited to the confinement of prison life. He described the morning ritual of the prison:

The wooden wall defined the southwest corner of the prison, 1886.

The grey streaks of dawn piercing the gloomy precincts of the vacant corridors; the dismal creak and crank of the tramping night guard upon the iron gallery, making his final round just before daylight, and sundry noises from all parts of the immense cell building announce the approach of day to the weary convict— weary of the night's dismal length and harrowing dreams—till the pandemonial summons recalls them to the hard legal fact of another day of hum-drum, diabolical, penal servitude.

He was desperate to get out any way he could. To set his plan in motion, he gained the confidence of Warden Stordock by saying he wanted to spend his evenings putting his writing skills to good use—teaching literacy courses to the inmates and gathering material for the Prison Mirror. He was granted access to the prison corridors until 8:30 P.M., a full hour after most prisoners were locked in their cells. In fact, Landers was looking for a private place where he could work his way through the bars and gain access to the prison yard. He found just such a place in the prison barbershop. Landers convinced Oscar J. Carlon, the prison barber, to join the plot, even though he had less than four months remaining on his sentence.

On October 6, Landers wrote an article for the *Prison Mirror* that revealed how deeply he despised his fellow inmates and the system that confined him. He complained that every man in the prison claimed to be innocent and to prove his reform reported on his fellow inmates:

> They should never have been sent here at all, so they thought. I think so, too, for they contaminated the decent thieves and made them worse. That is, they made me worse, for I never thought of murder till I became acquainted with such men.

The manly, business-like crook who simply follows the business he was educated to and takes his medicine as the square merchant does his losses, who stands up and says, "I did it, and I'll take the punishment; make it light as you can"—that kind of man never goes back to prison if he gets anything like a fair show to stay out. Sometimes, however, he becomes disgusted and tired, and says, "Well, I guess since I've got the name I may as well have some of the game." Look out for him then, Mr. Editor; he has become a bad man. But in all his career, from the hell that was his home to his last day in prison, you never hear him say, "If I had a fair trial I never would have been here," because the fact is, he never had any trial at all.

On October 12, the article appeared in the *Prison Mirror* and was distributed throughout the prison by editor W. F. Myrick and the prison librarian, Cole Younger. On that very night, Landers waited until 7:30 P.M., when Carlon shaved his last customer of the day and most inmates were being locked into their cells. Landers and

Carlon used a crowbar to bend one of the window bars enough that they could slip through into the prison yard. Once there, they went to the section of the prison wall constructed only of wooden boards and pried one of the planks loose. Their coats, apparently too bulky to slide through the bars, were discovered the next morning on the barbershop floor.

After Landers and Carlon escaped, the *Stillwater Democrat* reported on November 5, 1887:

> Every detective agency not only in the United States but also in Canada has [Landers's] description and portrait. The photograph of the noted criminal can be seen in every rogue's gallery in the country, and as he is wanted for so very many offenses at different places, his recovery is only a question of time, and perhaps only a few months may elapse before he is returned to the Minnesota authorities.

Although Carlon was soon recaptured, and time for his escape was tacked onto his sentence, Landers remained a fugitive. In March 1888, he was spotted in Chicago by Pinkerton agents, but when they learned that the reward for his capture was only $100, they let him go, not considering him worth the trouble. He was never returned to Stillwater. According to Carlon, Landers was headed for England.

COPYCAT ESCAPE ATTEMPTS

The success of Landers's escape inspired a number of imitators in the months that followed. None adhered to Landers's example more exactly than C. M. Morton. Unfortunately for Morton, the barred windows and wooden wall were replaced after Landers escaped; he was forced to be more industrious. On August 2, 1888, the *Stillwater Democrat* reported:

> On Saturday afternoon, a convict named C. M. Morton, under a ten-year sentence for larceny, attempted to escape from the state prison by digging through an eight inch brick wall, which separates the room from the water closet beneath the stairs under the main prison entrance hall. He had nearly completed an aperture large enough to admit of the passage of his body when discovered, and was promptly placed in the dungeon.

Debating Race

"Will a Negro Steal?"
Walter Turner, #2443

Turner, an African American man from Kentucky, was committed to Stillwater on February 5, 1887, to serve a two-year sentence for second-degree grand larceny. On October 12, 1887, he published an article in the Prison Mirror, *attempting to justify the theft that had landed him in prison.*

"There should be no pretext touching the anxiety of the colored man," said Cleveland in his inaugural address, neither should they be permitted to monopolize the columns of *The Mirror*, especially when they do not write anything worth reading. Every six months is often enough to hear from the few Negroes that are here, and not then

Unidentified inmates, 1890s, photographed for unknown reasons

unless interesting instead of trying to get into a rat hole. They are inclined to keep themselves before the readers of *The Mirror*. Their articles, like some of their white brothers, all have the same tone—mainly that of deception and "I-am-sorry-I-did-it." Any man with common sense can tell the truth from a lie. There is another feature about these articles. They all plead bad company, whisky and women. This is a very poor plea, for if everybody pleads bad company, where, then, is the bad company? This does not excuse them. The question is, are you going to do better or not? Will you steal or not? Make your decision now.

Some people think it very wrong to steal, especially in the United States, where their faulty idea of honor has a tendency to make a man steal. I hold that any man is justified in stealing if he is

89

in need, and when a man is in need that which he wants is as much his as it is anyone's. This I call honest stealing, and when a prisoner is brought up he should not be asked if he is guilty—he should plead guilty if he is guilty—and the court should ascertain why he stole and whether he had need of what he stole and help him to a job somewhere. If he steals again, burn a brand on his back, and if he steals again shoot him dead.

Some weeks ago a Negro preacher in Tennessee stole a cow to pay off a mortgage on his church. They put him in prison, of course; but was it right? No, a thousand times, no! for he had the right to steal a cow to redeem his church. And so I hold the Negro to be an honest man, for he has no ambition, and all he steals is something to eat, this being all he wants. I am glad that I am a Negro, and if all the Negroes that are in prison in the south for stealing hogs, corn, chickens and sweet potatoes were set at liberty, there would not be many left. Who will be the first to start this movement? I'd hasten to Egypt, interview the governors, after which their actions would be great, for they would forthwith pardon all niggers that are in for stealing something to eat; and God would let those governors pass, their actions he would exonerate.

"Race Love"
Sam Jones, #2271

Jones, also an African American inmate serving a four year sentence for second-degree grand larceny, responded angrily to Turner's article in the Prison Mirror, *October 19, 1887.*

We often hear of dog eating dog, but when it comes to Negro eating Negro, it's a little contrary to the enlightenment of the 19th century. The author of "Will a Negro Steal?" is a Negro who, some years ago, while hoeing in the waving cornfields of Kentucky, became tired from toil and laid down under a shady tree to sleep. While sleeping he had a dream. Lo, as it were, a man appeared to him with tidings of great joy. "Get thee up out of this land, for thou art anointed to be a great poet." So we find he has left his old Kentucky home far away behind him, and instead of the hoe he has grasped the pen. A sword in the hands of an infant is dangerous only to the holder. So I say a pen in the hands of a Kentucky dreamer is dangerous to him only. Allow me to tell you, my refined fellow convict Walter Turner, that you are twenty years behind the times; that while you were sleeping in the corn fields of Kentucky, the 13th, 14th, and 15th amendments have brought your nation to the sublime landmark of education and learning. Furthermore, that you are not in Kentucky now, and that you are across the Mason and Dixon line many miles; perhaps you don't know it.

What do you know about Cleveland or what does Cleveland or the democratic party know about you? They, as a party, know us as their slaves or hirelings; they underrate us. Knowing them only as masters we overrate them. They regard us as spiritless and mean. We regard them as cruel and blood-thirsty. In their eyes we are dishonest; in ours they are hypocrites and robbers. To a larger extent than either believes, both are mistaken; each is more human than the other thinks.

So take my advice and go back to Kentucky, for you are out of your latitude. Your gift as a scholar is no good and your dream lied to you. Your ignorance is "bliss," not to you, but the dream, and I suppose your wisdom has taught you that chickens roost higher in Minnesota than they do in Kentucky, and that your would-be wit is not appreciated. Napoleon said to his brave legions in glittering array, "Remember, the eyes of Europe are upon you."

Colored people should remember that the eyes of mankind are upon them. The colored man is on trial before the world, and so long that such Negroes exist, as the one before me, they will ever be convicted. The colored man has a task never before imposed upon a race beneath the stars. Races have fought wars of conquest; races have fought to establish and extripate religions; races have fought to throw off the yoke of tyrants; races have fought for personal liberty— but no race ever had to combat the combined sentiment of mankind to establish its character. The colored race is fighting for all that makes life dear, on earth or in heaven. Shall we prove equal to the momentous demands of our day and generation, or disgracefully, ignominiously fail? Yes, if any more of the Kentucky dreamers come to the front with their sickening articles, we'll fail. So take my advice and instead of going to Egypt, go back to Kentucky where the chickens roost low, and the sun shines hot; for in Egypt there are no chickens or sweet potatoes and they hang a Negro for trying to be wise, and cry "well done."

The Hole

George L. Bartlett, #4342

When a prisoner was placed in a punishment cell, he was stripped of his clothing, given a third grade outfit and handcuffed to the barred door of a cell and a wooden door closed in front of the barred door which he stood facing. If he was tall, he did not have to reach above his shoulders to get his hands through the cross bars where he rested his wrists. If he was short, he was very much out of luck, as he was all but strung up by the wrists.

The furnishings in the punishment cells were a wooden plank, two by six feet, to sleep on, and a night bucket. No blankets were allowed and no opportunity to wash. Every morning at seven o'clock the prisoner was chained up to the door and at twelve o'clock noon, the prisoner was let down, when he was given one slice of bread and one cup of water. At one o'clock he was chained up again and kept there until six, when he was let down for the night. The one slice of bread at noon each day was all that he was given to eat. The doctor was immediately advised when a man was placed in punishment and visited him each day to see how he was standing the gaff.

This punishment, with reduction to the third grade, which always follows, was severe in the extreme. The principal offenses were "insolence and back talk to an officer" or "fighting," for which prisoners were placed in the "hole," as it was termed. A prisoner was not supposed to display his temper under any circumstances. When he did, the prisoner was put in the "hole" for it.

Inmates in solitary confinement at the State Reformatory, like those at the State Prison, were handcuffed to their cell doors.

Eight Days in the Hole
Walter Turner, #2443

Turner was confined to solitary from November 3 to November 11, 1887, just days after his debate with Sam Jones, for "complaining of his food." This unusually harsh punishment may have been due to the fact that Turner was African American. At the request of Warden Reed, Turner published this account in the Prison Mirror *in order to "tell the 'boys' as best I can, briefly, about the dungeon, better known to some of them as the 'hole,' more as a warning than anything else."*

The hole is, or is supposed to be, a clean, dark cell, with the barest necessities of life, where a man may, if he can, walk all night to keep from sleeping and sleep all day to keep from eating, and it is best to do this way, too, when you are in there, for the bed bugs will make you cry out, "O Lord, what must I do to be saved?" if you try to sleep at night. I walked until I almost fell; then I would take the bucket top and make down my bed in the corner and sleep awhile. When I awoke I "took up my bed and walked" again for fear the bed bugs would get it. Bed bugs in the hole? Well you just bet there is, and plenty of them, too. It is their headquarters.

On arising in the morning you must take the cup in one hand and pour out the water into the other over the bucket and wash your eyes, at least, for if you don't they will get sore. You can wipe your face on the front apron of your shirt. Do this night and morning. If you have any tobacco lay it up over the door at night, thereby fooling the bugs, or you will get them into your mouth.

Our Savior said when on earth that man should not live by bread alone. But they ignore that fact when they put you in the hole, for it is plain that while in there if you don't live on bread you will not live at all. Job says that "Man born of woman is of a few days and full of trouble." This means that he is full of vanity, whisky and wind. But I have to tell you that while in the hole you are full of water and nothing more, although kind-hearted Jake looks at you when he brings the water as if he would bring something else if he could. There is just two classes of men who can stand the hole. They are those who have full control over their minds and those who were practically born in holes. If you can keep your mind off food you will get on all right.

There are three dungeons in a row—A, B and C—and as luck would have it I was in the middle one, and I had plenty of company, such as the banging on the walls when we got our meager slices of bread. If you are familiar with the gallery promenaders you can tell what time it is.

The librarian was showing some ladies around the Sunday I was in there and when they got in front of my cell he said to them: "These are the dungeons." One of them fainted, as usual, and cried out, "The dungeon!" The librarian says: "Although I never had any experience myself, I have known a man to stay in there for six days." This made me feel better, for I thought that if that was all I would soon be out. Alas, to my dis-appointment, I found that my time had just begun. I tried one day to make Mr. Colligan and Jake feel good by asking them to let me out, and you ought to have seen them laughing in their sleeves as they were closing the door, but that night they brought me a larger piece of bread, and Jake was very generous with his water.

My losses while in the hole amount to 270 cents, six days good time, eight pounds of flesh, 27 meals, the privilege of writing home last Sunday, my good prison name and prestige; besides, I have a very bad cold and my clothes don't fit me. Those who contemplate a visit to the hole should apply for further information.

GOING BAD, GOING STRAIGHT

A Guard is Stabbed

With many inmates, the severity of prison punishments like solitary confinement had the opposite of their desired effect. Instead of subduing violent inmates, harsh treatment pushed some to go to brutal lengths in order to avoid being sent to "the hole." Such vicious episodes became legendary among prisoners and guards alike. When discussing instances of violence against prison guards, former inmate Samuel A. Phillips wrote:

> According to one of the stock stories carried along a number of years ago, one of the guards annoyed one of the inmates at the table and the aforesaid inmate, who had been hectored, worried, and annoyed

The dining room, where the attack took place

into partial insanity, jumped up and slashed the guard with a short, sharp shoe knife, greatly disfiguring him for life and blinding him in one eye.

This was more than a stock story; it was based in fact, but Phillips's version of the story had been turned around by fifteen years of cell house rumor and retelling, until the story no longer resembled the truth.

In fact, on September 8, 1896, guard Martin Powers was attacked in the dining room by inmate James Rogan. The following day, the *Stillwater Daily Gazette* reported:

> At dinner James Rogan suddenly rose and drawing his knife, made a lunge at Mr. Powers, who was standing close by

him. He struck twice, cutting two long gashes, one reaching from the forehead crossing the left eye and the nose, to the right cheek, and the other a little lower down, square across the face and cutting the tip of his nose. Rogan then followed up his attack by throwing a bottle of vinegar at the guard, but this his victim managed to dodge.

James Rogan, about 1900

Deputy Warden Frank H. Lemon subdued Rogan by beating him down with his cane and ordering him taken to solitary confinement. Warden Wolfer informed the prison managers that it was "feared that he will lose the sight of one of his eyes in consequence of the injury." Indeed, Powers did lose sight in his left eye, but he remained a guard in the prison system for another forty years. Rogan was again confined to solitary in June 1898 for "making threats against Mr. Powers." Nevertheless, when he finally retired in 1935, Powers remembered:

That fellow Rogan who assaulted me in 1896 wasn't a bad fellow at all. I never had him under me, but it came out in his trial in district court that he had been put up to the job by a man who resented me when he was working in the threshing machine shops.

Martin Powers, 1908. He lost all vision in his left eye after the brutal attack by James Rogan.

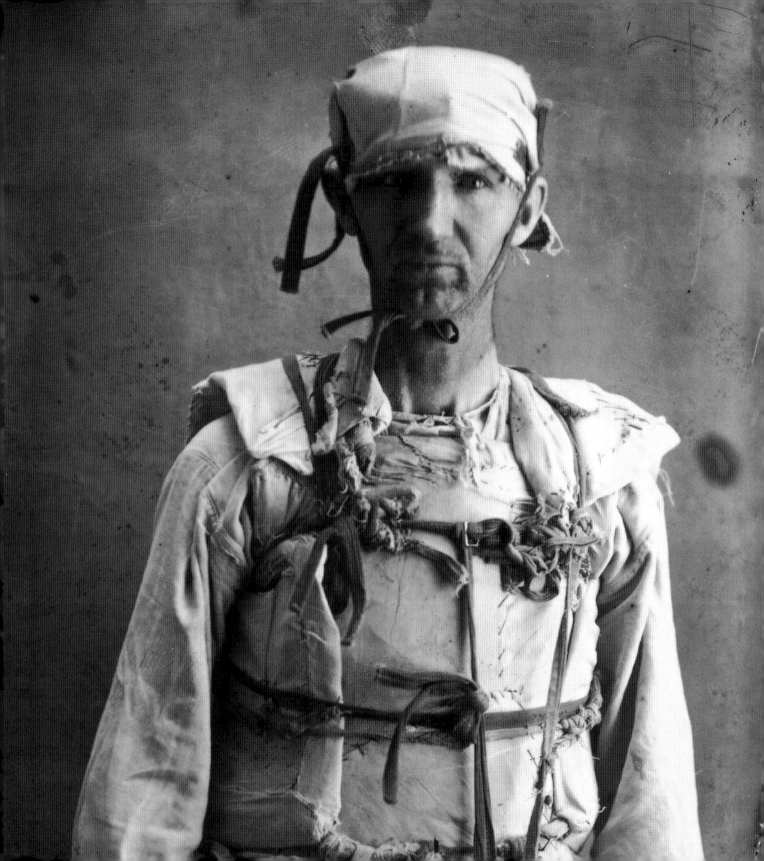

Insane Inmates

Warden Henry Wolfer

By the mid 1890s, the increasing size of the prison population made it difficult to deal with problem inmates. The most troublesome of all were mentally ill inmates. Guards disliked dealing with them, because they were unpredictable and often violent, but the hospital staff was ill equipped to handle them.

There is a strong and growing prejudice on the part of the officers of our insane hospitals against admitting insane criminals to their hospitals for treatment. They feel that it is an injustice to associate them in treatment with other patients for obvious reasons. I think the state should provide a special ward for these unfortunates, in connection with one of our insane hospitals, where they can receive suitable treatment, and at the same time be surrounded with conditions that will safely guard against any danger of escape. As a rule, insane criminals are possessed with a degree of low cunning, that requires close watching and careful guarding to prevent escape. This has been demonstrated several times, by the escapes already made from our insane hospitals.

As an instance, I will cite the case of Michael Brennan, who has been twice committed to the insane asylum. He is very dangerous most of the time, having strong homicidal tendencies. He escaped from Rochester, going south, and after considerable trouble and expense was finally captured at New Orleans, and was brought back to this prison. We have been obliged to keep him in close confinement most of the time since.

Mentally ill inmates were often restrained with primitive protective equipment. This unidentified photograph may show how they were outfitted.

The Twine Shop Insurrection

On July 20, 1899, a violent outbreak occurred in what came to be known as the twine shop insurrection. Three days earlier, a new guard named Conroy had been assigned to the spinning room of the prison twine shop. Inmate Charles Wilson recognized Conroy right away; Wilson had assaulted him years before when the guard had been a policeman in Minneapolis. Over the next two days, Conroy wrote up Wilson for several minor offenses, including looking around the shop and passing notes to his co-workers. On July 19, Wilson's friend W. E. Andrews enlisted the support of other inmates, promising "if somebody should start to fight, the fellows would get in and give him a licking."

After the attack, prison officials interviewed all the men who were in the twine shop that day.

The twine shop supervisor, at far left, oversaw dozens of inmate workers with nothing more than a wooden cane for defense.

William E. Andrews, #4957

Wilson asked permission to go to the water closet and after getting the pass spoke to the guard. I was then standing at Wilson's machine, I having relieved him in order for him to go to the closet. The guard spoke to him as he was passing by.

Charles Wilson, #4583

When the guard called me up and spoke to me about walking around the shop, I told him that if he reported me for this we would have trouble. When I said this, I squared off putting myself in a position to strike, and in a loud threatening manner, shaking my fist in his face, I told him what I would do. Then he struck me with a cane and I clinched him and the trouble began. He struck me the second time but dropped his cane.

William E. Andrews

They scuffled about in the center of the shop gradually working through the archway into the opposite shop from where I was located. As they went down I went up to where the trouble was and said to the other prisoners, "Get in fellows, now is the time." At this juncture several others said in threatening tones, "Get off him, get off him," and I hit the guard on the side of the head.

Charles Wilson

Andrews's blow staggered the guard very much and as we were about to fall convict Ross, #5008, struck the guard in the back of the head with a piece of iron and the guard and I fell to the floor, the guard falling on top of me. At this point convicts Frank Lewis, #4738, and Roberts, who works in the middle row of spinners in Shop E

James Ross, #5088

between Ross and Howard, came up. They, together with Andrews, threatened the guard, telling him that if he touched me what they

would do, told him to let me up, told the guard Conroy that if he touched me they would knock his goddamn head off.

J. C. Davis, #5117

The blow from Ross stunned the officer, and Haggerty pulled Ross away. Ross appeared anxious to hit the officer again. I think the guard said, "You fellows go on back to your work." I did not hear anything else. At this point I struck the guard in the head with a weight, which I took from the top of one of the spinners which fits down in the nipper with a ball on top of it. I stepped back to the machine and took this implement and struck him on the right side of the head, a glancing blow with an upward cut.

Charles Wilson

This cut the guard's head badly and he bled very hard, blood running over my shoulder and down the guard's face. The guard's face was turned towards the men threatening to assault him when Davis came up behind and gave him the ripping blow.

J. C. Davis

Immediately after hitting the guard, I dropped the weight on the carrier of the same spinner I took it out of, before returning to my work, but just as I dropped the weight on the machine, Deputy Warden Alexander came into the shop. As he walked in, I saw him make a motion with his hands, and the prisoners scattered all going back to their work.

The men who participated in this brutal attack were given from three to five days in solitary confinement. No time was added to their sentences.

HENRY WOLFER, WARDEN.
J. S. GLENNON, DEPUTY WARDEN.
H. W. DAVIS, CLERK.
F. M. BORDWELL, STEWARD.

MINNESOTA STATE PRISON.

Stillwater, Minn. Jan. 3, 1903.

Chas. J. Moos, Esq.,

Clerk Board of Pardons,

St. Paul, Minn.

Dear Sir:-

Replying to your inquiry of the 2nd inst., in behalf of the Honorable Board of Pardons regarding the merits of application for executive clemency of Thomas Coleman Younger, with information as to his behavior since his release on parole, the condition of his health, etc., I beg leave to report that, so far as I have been able to find out his conduct has been above reproach in every respect. I believe that he has done his best to fulfill every requirement since his parole. As to his health, it has been bad for some years covering a considerable period before as well as since his release on parole. His physical disability has been caused by kidney troubles and by the formation of gall stones in his bladder. His age and physical condition is such that it is difficult for him to earn a livlihoood unaided.

I believe it would be an act of charity and mercy to Younger and at the same time for the benefit of the State and the community at large if a conditional pardon might be granted him, upon such lines as the Honorable Board of Pardons in its wisdom might think best.

Respectfully submitted,

MINNESOTA STATE PRISON,

Henry Wolfer

WARDEN

MAS COLEMAN YOUNGER FOR

L PARDON AS THE BOARD MA

uant to one of the

anted to me,

hat I will never

ted, as an actor

eum, circus,

blic amuse-

mission. This

such public

A.D.1903.

unger,

Parole: The Star of Hope

Cole Younger, #700

Shortly after his arrival at the prison in 1892, Warden Wolfer instituted a system of "conditional pardons," granted by the governor, by which certain convicts would be allowed to leave the prison upon pledging to adhere to strict rules on the outside. Violations would lead to reincarceration. The system was effective enough that a state agent was hired to supervise paroled prisoners, but it did not help Cole Younger.

The parole system provided by the enlightened humanitarianism of the state for other convicts did not apply to lifers. Under this system a convict whose prison record is good may be paroled on his good behavior after serving half of the term for which he was sentenced.

After two years on parole, Younger was recommended for a pardon by Warden Wolfer.

In the legislature of 1899, our friends endeavored to have the parole system extended to life prisoners, and secured the introduction in the legislature of a bill to provide that life prisoners might be paroled when they had served such a period as would have entitled them to their release had they been sentenced to imprisonment for thirty-five years.

As the good time allowances on a thirty-five-year sentence would cut it to between twenty-three and twenty-four years, we could have been paroled in a few months had this bill passed. Although there was one other inmate of the prison who might have come under its provisions, it was generally known as the "Youngers' parole bill" and the feeling against it was largely identified with the feeling against us.

Still it did not discourage our friends on the outside.

At the next session of the legislature, 1901, there was finally passed the bill which permitted our conditional parole, the pardon board not being ready to grant us our full freedom. This bill provided for the parole of any life convict who had been confined for twenty years, on the unanimous consent of the board of pardons.

The board of prison managers promptly granted the parole, the principal conditions of which were as follows:

He shall not exhibit himself in any dime museum, circus, theater, opera house, or any other place of public amusement or assembly where a charge is made for admission.

He shall on the twentieth day of each month write the warden of the state prison a report of himself, stating whether he had been constantly at work during the last month, and if not, why not; how much he had earned, and how much he has expended, together with a general statement as to his surroundings and prospects, which must be indorsed by his employer.

He shall in all respects conduct himself honestly, avoid evil associations, obey the law, and abstain from the use of intoxicating liquors.

He shall not go outside the state of Minnesota.

And July 14, 1901, Jim and I went out into the world for the first time in within a few months of twenty-five years. Rip Van Winkle himself was not so long away.

THE SUICIDE OF JIM YOUNGER
Cole Younger, #700

After our release from prison, Jim's precarious health and his inability to rejoin his family in Missouri combined to make these fits of depression more frequent. In July, some of his friends petitioned the board of pardons for a full pardon, but the board was of the opinion that it was too early to consider. That resulted in another fit of depression for Jim. He took it to heart, and never regained his cheerful attitude. On October 19, his dead body was found in a room at the hotel Reardon. A bullet hole above his right ear and a pistol clutched in his hand, told the story of suicide.

PAROLED PRISONERS
F. A. Whittier, State Agent

As a companion to his program of parole, Warden Wolfer created the position of state agent, now called a parole officer, who would find work for and supervise the lives of parolees in order to monitor their progress in the outside world. "With continued friendly oversight and encouragement," Wolfer wrote, inmates showed remarkable progress toward reform.

Paroled prisoners are required to report to me in writing once a month, which report is in the form of questions and answers and gives in detail their earnings, how same was spent, where and how their leisure time was spent, the general character of their reading, etc., which report is countersigned by their employer. Of the 101 prisoners, eight have violated their parole agreement, six of whom have been returned to prison, and two are still at large. Of the eight who have violated their parole, five have done so by using intoxicating liquors, and three by moving away from their place of employment. Only one is known to have committed a crime while on parole, and in his case the crime was committed in order to secure means to escape, he having broken his parole previously. I have made it a practice to call upon these men on parole as often as possible, in order to strengthen them in their efforts towards good citizenship. These friendly visits occupy much of my time, and I believe are quite essential. In making them I have traveled 19,780 miles by rail, and believe that the good accomplished is worth the effort. In most cases I am received in a friendly way, and they seem to understand that we are trying to help them and are quite willing to avail themselves of our help. I found when I assumed this position that the parole law was very little understood by the general public, and considerable of my time has been spent in explaining the law and showing what we are trying to do for these men; and I am happy to say that the good people of this state are quite willing, when they have fully understood our efforts, to help us in this work.

Reward poster for Mike Radovac, issued May 28, 1909. While on parole, he shot State Agent Whittier and made his getaway.

The Escape of McCarty and Juhl

From the Stillwater Daily Gazette, March 6, 1911

Jerry McCarty and Peter Juhl, a pair of convicts from Minneapolis, made their escape from the state prison on Saturday night early. They are still at large and the prison authorities have no definite clue as to their whereabouts. The surrounding country was scoured by prison guards and others Saturday night.

From the best obtainable information and deductions from known facts the men made their escape from their cell house on tier one about 8 o'clock Saturday evening. It is believed that McCarty either made a key or was supplied with one by outside confederates.

The key is supposed to have been given to Juhl by McCarty, when the former, as a trusty, was on his rounds with the torch to light the paper wafers of the convicts; he timed affairs so as to unlock the bar that runs along the front of the cell doors, while the guards were at the other end of the corridor. This was unlocked and gently raised, McCarty opened his cell door and they walked rapidly away to liberty.

Then they went to the stone wall together, just north of the railway gate at the north end of the prison. There they scaled the wall by climbing upon the gates, and dropped to the sidewalk on the outside. The men were missed in a few minutes. The prison whistle summoned guards and clerks that had left for the day and the chase commenced.

Guards, often using bloodhounds, were called from the Minnesota State Reformatory and other state lock-ups to join police and private detectives in the manhunt.

The Capture of Jerry McCarty
Minneapolis Journal, July 16, 1911

Jerry McCarty, #2908

In a revolver battle at close range, Jerry McCarty, escaped convict and known as one of the most desperate criminals in America, and Patrolman Joseph Ollinger killed each other last night at Central and Twenty-fifth avenue NE. The hunted man, cornered, did just what his pursuer expected him to do, opened the first fire. Ollinger fired almost at the same instant. McCarty fell first and Ollinger, with four bullets in his body, fell on him.

The battle, which eclipses any in the annals of the Minneapolis police, ends a search for McCarty which has extended throughout the United States, while McCarty, who had escaped from Stillwater penitentiary on March 4, continued his career of robbery.

Ollinger had seen McCarty hanging about pool rooms in the New Boston district for several days. Early yesterday, after a conference with Ollinger, Captain of Detectives Nick Smith said Ollinger had the right man.

Kissing his wife goodbye, Ollinger said as he left home yesterday, "There may be something doing tonight," and then left to go on his night watch.

From that moment he was after McCarty. He saw McCarty at Central avenue and Twenty-fourth avenue and followed him slowly to Twenty-fifth avenue. There McCarty turned and walked along Twenty-fifth avenue to the rear of Harry Bussum's drug store. The fugitive stopped at the rear entrance and Ollinger turned into the store.

"McCarty is at your back door and I'm going to get him," said Ollinger to Bussum. "There's going to be trouble." Then he walked straight to McCarty and said, "McCarty, I've got you now or you've got me."

Then McCarty opened fire and Ollinger followed. Each man emptied the chambers of his revolver almost in a second. Just as the firing ceased, McCarty fell with a bullet through his heart and Ollinger, shot six times through the body, fell on him. Both men died of their wounds.

The Capture of Peter Juhl
***Minneapolis Journal*, August 13 and 14, 1911**

Peter Juhl, #3085

Detective Frank Fraser of St. Paul, one of the best known police officers in the twin cities and hero of many gun fights with desperate criminals was shot on a crowded Selby-Lake car. His assailant, who gave the name of Arthur Lewis after the shooting was indentified as Peter Juhl, companion of Jerry McCarty in a sensational escape from the state prison at Stillwater last March. The shooting was in the front of the car in view of fifty passengers who became terror stricken and rushed for the doors, paying no heed to the wounded detective's calls for help.

Fraser, who has a keen eye for police description, had arrested Juhl on the car after following him from the wholesale millinery establishment of S. Weiss & Co. A circular sent out by a millinery association warned wholesalers to look out for thieves who inspect the stores before robbing them. Juhl entered the place and Weiss, who had read the description of a man wanted, suspected him. He called the police and Fraser was sent.

Fraser followed and boarded the car right behind Juhl. Fraser told the conductor that he was going to arrest the man. He walked to the front of the car, where Juhl had gone, and sat in the seat beside him.

"You are under arrest," said Fraser quietly.

Juhl jumped up in his seat and reached for his revolver. Knowing what the move meant Fraser stood up, grasped Juhl by the neck and bent him over the seat in front. Juhl obtained his revolver, pressed it against Fraser's body and fired. The first shot entered the abdomen, but Fraser grasped the revolver, turned it away and the second shot went through his hand.

Though wounded and suffering intense pain Fraser clung to his prisoner, who still held the smoking revolver in his hand, until Patrolman Michael Fallon boarded the car, felled Juhl with his club and helped the wounded man from the car. After Fraser's death Juhl was at once taken to municipal court and arraigned on a charge of murder. He will face a life imprisonment charge.

A Place in the Printing Office

Samuel A. Phillips, #2479

Samuel A. Phillips was a well-established accountant working for a number of Minnesota railroads when he was found guilty of embezzling funds. On the afternoon of August 13, 1908, the last of Phillips's repeated appeals failed, and two deputy sheriffs were dispatched to find him. When they arrived at his office door, Phillips asked, "Bad news?" and one of the deputies replied, "Yes, very bad." They cuffed him and took him directly to Stillwater.

Presently the Deputy Warden arrived. He said: "Follow me." No sooner had I entered his office than he yelled at me in stentorian tones that shook the building, "Fold your arms." Then, "Sit over there!" He pointed to a box and

Composing room for the *Prison Mirror*, about 1910

I sat down. With the aid of his convict clerk he took my "pedigree" and finally inquired: "What's yer trade?" I said I was a printer by trade, but had not worked at it for twenty-five years. He then said: "Wait here until I come back. They may need a printer down in the print shop. I will go down and see the editor and find out." I waited about a half hour. He came back and said: "Yes, they need a man in the printun' offus and I'm goin' to give ye a chance. The editor is a crank, but try and git along with him." I said I would do the best I could and was introduced to the editor who immediately put me at work setting type and said he would like to have me write a couple of columns of stuff weekly for the prison paper, the *Mirror*. The boys in the printing office received me very graciously. They tried to make things as agreeable as they could. As soon as they got a favorable opportunity to talk during the absence of the editor they expressed their great sympathy and said they were familiar with the case and thought it a great outrage I was sent there. One fellow said: "We are all crooks and belong here for a while any way, but it is different with you—you were robbed by the interests and every one familiar with the facts knows it."

In reply to all that I said: "My attorney expects to get me out before long." They all laughed. One fellow said: "That's an old story with us. Every fresh fish landed here expects to get out right away because his lawyer says so. Mouthpieces (lawyers) can't do a fellow much good after he once lands here behind the bars." "Yes," broke in another, "They don't catch a sucker like you every week or month and now that you are here if you get two years taken off your sentence you will be lucky or I miss my guess."

Later the editor informed me that a place had been held open for me for several weeks in the printing office despite the fact that there were other printers the place who had arrived ahead of me.

In the printing office everything went along all right. I was setting as much type as any of my compatriots in durance vile and contributed some weeks as many as nine columns of matter, such as it was, to the family journal. I was in total darkness so far as news from the outside world was concerned. Quite a few friends called to see me, but I discouraged calling as much as I could for the reason that I did not care to have friends or relatives see me in prison costume.

To a new arrival the guards are fierce, and I was no exception to the rule. I was yelled at as, "Hey, you," told to climb the stairs more rapidly and all that sort of thing. Upon entering the prison I weighed 240 pounds stripped and soon lost thirty-five pounds, which I was very glad to do. I had been trying every means to reduce, except the proper one, that of living on very plain food and not much of it.

At the closet one day a contributor to the *Mirror* stopped me and complained of the poor proof reading on his five-column story that week in the *Mirror*. I told him I had nothing to do with it and I was reported and sent to court again, the third time in three weeks.

The Deputy Warden gave me a bawling out which I would be ashamed to repeat. He also said: "You've got a sixteen candlepower electric globe

Editor's room for the *Prison Mirror*, about 1910

in yer cell. If I'd a known about it, ye wouldn't a-had it." I said, "I did not get it surreptitiously," and then the fur flew, for he did not know whether I was cursing him in Esperanto or not. However, I escaped with my life and my spirit was broken all right. I never imagined persons could be so contemptible.

When I went back to the printing office the boys asked me about it and I told them. One fellow said: "Talking is all right if you do not get caught, but if the officers catch you talking they will raise hell with you. Its a damned shame," continued this fellow, "but they will let you alone after a while when they *think* they have your spirit

broken. It is the old story," he continued, "'It is not that I hate ye that I bate ye, but just to show me authority—dom ye,' but it is not necessary to be so fierce." Four marks in six months will detain an inmate from reaching the first grade on time and as first-grade prisoners are permitted to write a letter every week instead of one every other week, the average prisoner is very anxious to reach the goal promptly on schedule.

The next week I was reported for being late out of my cell. I was late, not over two seconds, however. I was sent to court. Same old scowl, same old grimace, same old fierce admonition.

About a week later I was jackassed up to court on the heinous charge of breaking bread instead of cutting it. When I appeared before the Deputy Warden and the accusation was read to me I denied it. The guard who reported me was acting as Grand Marshal that day. He said: "I seen you do it." I said, "You are mistaken." "Well, there was gravy on it, any way." I was admonished and sent away. That guard from that time on pursued me with a venom and spitefulness that would not do credit to a mongrel cur or mutt.

Editing the Prison Mirror

Samuel A. Phillips, #2479

When I was appointed editor of the prison paper a great hue and cry went up among some of the lifers and old-timers that it was a shame the Warden had appointed "that fat slob editor—he ought to have appointed So-and-so or So-and-so," fellows who could not spell simple words, let alone write correctly. I tried to improve the paper and attend to the large amount of job-work to the best of my ability. Mr. John Carter, the famous prison poet who achieved a world-wide reputation through the *Mirror*, swung into line for two columns of good stuff each week, including prose and poetry. His stuff was a little too heavy for the average inmate, but it made a great hit with the better educated prisoners and on the outside of the prison among the readers of the

An unidentified inmate in the *Prison Mirror* office, about 1910

paper his contributions were considered marvelous. The editor of the *Mirror* is allowed the very widest latitude by the Warden along certain lines. Politics, personalities and religion are tabooed. Therefore, it is not an easy matter to produce a "live" paper every week. Mr. Carter's stuff was extraordinary and was so recognized to be by the best critics in the country.

Prisoners in other penal institutions have their poets, elocutionists and orators, but during the latter part of Mr. Carter's confinement there was no penal institution that stood as high all around from a literary point of view as the Minnesota State Prison, and the deduction to be derived is this: Prison life is no bar to the development of mental faculties under any sort of decent or half-way encouragement.

John Carter, Prison Poet

By the time John Carter was released from Stillwater on April 19, 1910, his story was national news. Carter had won a commutation of his sentence a full five years before his scheduled release, due largely to letters of appeal from the editors of the *Century*, *Cosmopolitan*, *Harper's Weekly*, and *Lippincott's*. Each had published poems by Carter and, at the urging of William Marion Reedy, an editor of the *St. Louis Mirror*, had petitioned the pardons board to consider his work as evidence of rehabilitation. When news broke that the board had granted Carter a pardon, the story was carried by newspapers from the *Los Angeles Times* to the *New York Evening Sun* to the *London Times* in Carter's native England. The *St. Paul Pioneer Press* ran the front-page headline, "Prison Poet is Free Man Today." The

Century offered Carter a position as a contributing writer, and Baker & Taylor agreed to publish Carter's prison house poetry in a volume entitled *Hard Labor and Other Poems*.

Carter's start in Minnesota was considerably less auspicious. After failing out of Weymouth College and coming to loathe his dead-end job as a bank clerk in London, Carter struck out at the age of nineteen for a new life of farming in Canada. "Behind me were friends and failure," he later remembered, "ahead merely an uncertain hope." He soon found a job as a hired hand on a farm in Elm Creek, Manitoba, near Winnipeg, but farm life didn't agree with Carter after all. "A bookworm on a farm is more out of place than a farm hand in a library," he wrote, so without asking for wages, he one day walked the

Canadian Northern rail line the sixty miles to Winnipeg. There he took a series of odd jobs—dishwasher, furniture mover, saloon pianist.

Hoping to find better work in St. Paul, Carter hopped an empty boxcar in the Winnipeg rail yard and road across the border into Minnesota, but shortly after sunrise he was discovered and thrown out near the small town of Karlstad. Officially, Karlstad wasn't even a town yet, just a train station and a handful of houses near the tracks. No one needed a hired hand, so Carter stood on the platform waiting for the next train. The station agent kept yelling at him to go away until Carter finally hid behind a row of boxcars, waiting for nightfall. Once the station agent and his wife went to sleep upstairs, Carter broke into the downstairs office, emptied the drawer of its twenty-four dollars, and fled town following the tracks.

By daybreak he had reached the next town and stumbled into a restaurant where he ordered "the most sumptuous meal a man ever had." He walked back down to the tracks but was too tired to run, and soon four men on a handcar caught up to him and put him under arrest. He was appointed a public defender who offered in Carter's defense only, "Your honor, the accused, John Carter is but 19 years old, and I therefore plead for a reformatory sentence." The judge couldn't believe he was only nineteen and refused to offer a sentence to the state reformatory. Instead, Carter was sentenced to the Minnesota State Prison at Stillwater for the mandatory term for burglarizing an occupied dwelling: ten years.

Hard Labor

I work, and as the task is done I brood
  On what has been and what is yet to pass,
  A life spilt from an idly-handled glass,
And days as this, an endless multitude.

Labor and brooding—is there then no rest?
  Day follows day, and in the silent nights
  Throng ghostly memories of past delights,
Faces I loved, and lips that I have pressed,

Until the sullen, deep-toned morning bell
  Wakes me to face a yesterday again
  With all its bitter agony of pain.
Thou didst not linger, Dante, in thy hell.

They say the torture's gone, the dawn's arisen,
  Mercy, to angered hearts a suitor strange,
  Has begged her own; yet this they cannot change,
I have been free, and I am here in prison.

The Unspeakable Realities of Confinement

Samuel A. Phillips, #2479

From 1911 to 1912, shortly after his release from Stillwater, Samuel A. Phillips published a series of anonymous articles in his magazine, The Monitor, *addressing several topics central to prison life but rarely discussed. For the time he was writing, many of these articles were extremely controversial. Among the taboo subjects he described were the high divorce rate among inmates, sex in the prison, and the overwhelming depression that often led to suicide.*

Divorce

No matter how vehemently or lovingly the average wife of a convicted man vows and swears she will remain true until his period of penance is over, nevertheless in five cases out of six the wife within two years, if the sentence of her husband be longer than that, will invariably begin an action for divorce and, of course, there is no defense. Volumes might be written upon this subject, but it is out of place right here. The worst blow that can come to a man in prison is to have his wife for whom he probably committed the crime for which he is imprisoned, go back on him, but it is the way of the world.

Divorces have not been so numerous, perhaps, in the Stillwater prison since the inmates have been "put on the payroll." Prisoners are paid as a rule fifteen cents a day, a certain stipend for overwork and so much per piece for extra production. This is a most beneficial law and while the wages are small they nevertheless count up in prison and as the inmates are fed, sheltered and

clothed they have the use of this money for the things they need and are permitted, such as good shoes, underwear, socks, eyeglasses and teeth repairs—also the purchase of books and papers, or the taking of a correspondence course in law, civil engineering, architecture or any other line of study desired. The married man in prison who can send his wife from $4.00 a month upward is contributing at least something to her support and a small amount of money coming from a prisoner goes a long way. I believe the passage of this law and its being put into effect in the Stillwater prison is the best thing that has ever been done in the history of the State of Minnesota affecting penological problems.

Sex

While I know absolutely nothing about it except from reliable hearsay, vile practices go on in the prison in spite of all the officers can do to watch it, but this crime-against-nature business is practiced by the rounders—those who started at the training schools and have passed through the reformatories and finally landed in prison. It is practiced only among the trusties, runners and favorites of the management who have exceptional advantages to meet in out-of-the-way places.

Whenever the officers catch any of the inmates practicing these nefarious and beastly Oscar Wilde rackets they are severely dealt with. I do not pretend to be too prudish to recognize such things and do all I can to stamp them out. I am fortyfive years of age. I came out of prison with rosy cheeks and in the best of health with the exception of my eyes and lungs being weak. There was not much prison pallor on me and I do not believe I had acquired the furtive glance of the long timer in prison.

Self-abuse is indulged in to some extent. Medical works are in possession of certain inmates in which it is claimed that self-abuse is a help to health when not indulged in to excess. Quite a few of the inmates are so lost to all shame and sense of decency that they boast of indulging in that sort of practice and some fellows whom the officers least suspect. I could generally spot those chaps. They had the prison pallor and their eyes looked fishy, dead and dull. Some of them would say to me, "You're looking fine—how do you do it?" I always responded to the effect that I was regular and straightforward in my habits. That was enough. They understood.

Suicide

I presume there are very few men who ever entered prison who did not at one time or another consider the advisability of ending their misery by their own hands, but along would come a decision of the Board of Pardons which would put renewed hope in their breasts and encourage them to live out their destinies. Prisoners, as a rule, encourage one another to "go through with" their sentences. Once in a while a couple of weak-minded chaps will get together and encourage each other to shuffle off this mortal coil by their own hands. Lifers and long-timers are given special advantages after they have been in prison a stated length of time and that is perfectly proper. The fellow who is "in" for a short time can stand it better than the chap who may never get out. The short-timer is buoyed up by the hope that his sentence is getting shorter. The lifer who is guilty—knows he is guilty—and knows that every one else familiar with his case knows it—has very little hope of getting any relief until he has served at least twenty years and then will probably be paroled.

The prisoners receive very little, if any, encouragement from the sub-officers. No friendly eye to greet them, ruled by a wave of the hand or a nod of the head, the prisoner, no matter how intelligent or industrious, is made to feel at all times the humiliation and degradation of his position, whether innocent or guilty and in my opinion there are many persons confined in the Stillwater penitentiary who do not belong there by any means. The sub-officials are very illiterate, having no education whatever and have no opportunity of improving themselves. Many of them admit they would not be prison guards if they could earn a livelihood at anything else. The prisoners all affect to be superior to the guards and say, "those guys are not half as good as I am or they wouldn't be screws in a stir." The average prisoner holds the guards in the greatest contempt on account of their meanness, smallness and general contemptibility in reporting them for trifles and sending them to court to be bawled out unmercifully by officers who are the ones who really need the daily admonishments they hand to others with a few exceptions.

Take a prisoner who is working hard, doing as much labor as a citizen on the outside, takes pride in his production and is sent to court for some little trifle for example, as gazing around in the dining room or something equally as silly and he becomes nervous for a week. His nervous sys-

tem gets a jolt and he cannot shake it off. If a prisoner viciously violates a rule and is sent to court he takes his medicine like a man. The accusation is frequently made by well-posted prisoners in Stillwater that the court system has caused not a few suicides. The tendency toward suicide in prison is marked. Under certain conditions the suicides are more numerous than at other times. The harshness of the subofficers has a good deal to do with making life so miserable for a prisoner that death is the only relief.

THE SUICIDE OF HENRY SUSSMAN

In late 1905, Henry Sussman shot his wife in the head and turned on the gas, intending to commit suicide. Before he asphyxiated, however, he was discovered by police and arrested. Sussman had been depressed long before the incident, at least since he learned that his wife, Fannie, worked occasionally as a prostitute. At his trial, Sussman was defended by the famed African American lawyer Fredrick L. McGhee, who mounted a rousing defense of temporary insanity, but the jury wasn't convinced. The defense, however, did show sufficient mitigating factors that Sussman was sentenced to life in prison, rather than death by hanging. On December 19, 1906, he was committed to Stillwater.

In the silent hours of the night in early March 1908, Sussman tore his pillowcase into strips and fashioned a cord. At six o'clock the following morning, he was found dead, hanging by the neck in his cell. The *Prison Mirror* reported that he "was sad and down-hearted from the day he was sentenced. The young man was a good prisoner and an excellent workman, and his death is a sad blow to his parents." One of the dead man's brothers claimed his remains and saw to his burial in Minneapolis. Henry Sussman was just twenty-one years old.

Henry Sussman, #2016

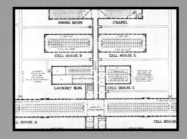

Plans for a New Prison

Handbook of the Minnesota State Prison, 1909

In 1905, the legislature appropriated funds for the planning of a new prison at a site a few miles south of Stillwater, in what is now Bayport. After four years of discussions and preliminary construction, the full plan for an ambitious and modern prison was unveiled in 1909.

The first Minnesota State Prison was a wooden building designed to accommodate about one hundred persons and was cut off from the outside world by a wooden fence, upon which at regular intervals were platforms for armed guards. The old prison has long since passed away to make room for the one now occupied.

The location of the present prison is poorly

The new prison at South Stillwater (now Bayport) about 1909, before the permanent concrete walls were erected

adapted to the purposes for which it is used owing to the inadequacy of the building and the insufficiency of ground in the enclosure, there being but nine and one-half acres all told. The cell-house particularly is far from being the proper kind of a building in which to house 700 inmates. The ventilation of the building is very bad and unhealthful to the inmates. The windows are small and narrow and the light and air are poor, thus endangering the health of the prisoners, sapping their energies unnecessarily and decreasing their manual efficiency.

The new prison is located two and one-half miles south of the present location of the old prison on a beautiful plateau overlooking the St. Croix river at an elevation of about forty feet. Directly in front of the new prison, the ground

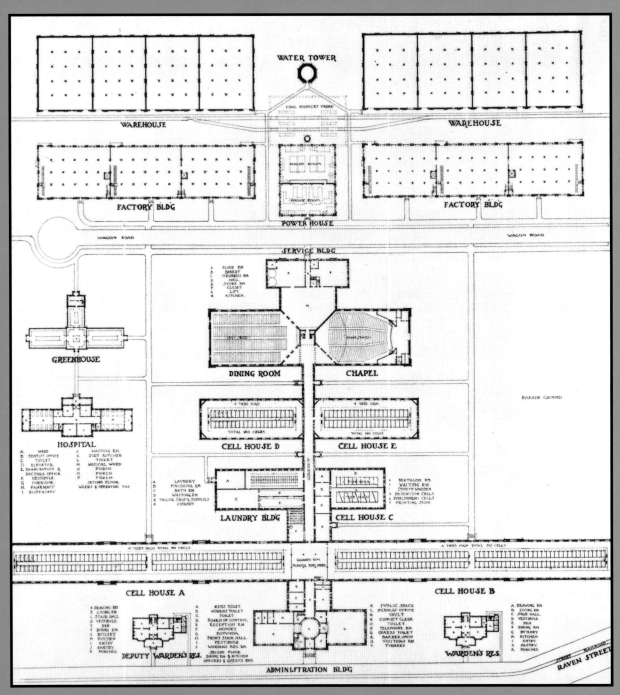

The ground plan of the new state prison, 1909

slopes abruptly to the river flats, thus affording a fine view of a picturesque character—not only to the prisoners but those outside.

The new prison at South Stillwater is reached by an electric line running from Stillwater and the service will be maintained at a high degree of efficiency as needed for the accommodation of visitors and those having business at the institution.

Walls constructed of reinforced concrete on three sides, north, south, and west, including the administration building on the east, will enclose the prison proper of twenty-two acres. From the administration building in the center two large cell houses A and B radiate at right angles, stretching clear across the front of the prison, one thousand feet in distance.

The plans for the new prison are in line with and abreast of the best thought on modern prison architecture, and when completed, will be one of the best and most modern prisons in the United States, if not in the world. The buildings will be plain, substantial, and comfortable, and while all the laws and rules for obtaining the best hygienic and sanitary conditions will be carefully followed, and all of the buildings made strictly fireproof, there will be no extravagant or unnecessary display. Most prisons in the United States are now taking from fifteen to twenty-five years in building. The best of them cost from three to four million dollars, the prisons are old and out-of-date, and cost much more than if built comprehensively and quickly, as is now planned in Minnesota.

The new prison ought to be built in four years, and certainly not later than five years.

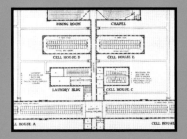

Ho for the New Prison

Prison Mirror, January 28, 1909

In 1909, when the new prison was still under construction, the slow movement of the inmate population from the old prison was begun. The intention was to move prisoners into the newer, more efficient twine factories as quickly as possible, in order to assure maximum production.

The transfer of the crew of men to the factory at the site for the new prison was made Monday morning. Each man had his belongings with him. The men were placed in two Northern Pacific passenger coaches in which several guards were stationed. The trip was without incident.

As the coaches passed through Stillwater, it was rumored that some citizens could be seen along the hillsides hiding their valuables, but this

Loading prisoners onto the transport train to the new prison, 1909

was unnecessary as the men were too interested in the trip to think of anything else.

Arriving at Oak Park, the men entered the fifteen foot board fence that surrounds the two factory buildings, and then were marched to the dormitory on the third floor of the building in which twine will be manufactured. A small crew of prisoners was put to work in the dormitory Sunday morning cleaning up the place, and they had everything in fine shape for occupancy.

R. M. Coles will have general charge at the new place, he being responsible for the discipline and safe custody of the inmates in his care. The prisoners at the new place will have their clothing washed here; also they will likely be furnished with books from the library. The twine factory will be started at once.

First engine leaving for the new prison, 1909

The makeshift railroad gate into the new prison, 1909

Unloading prisoners at the new prison, 1909

The turnkey's cage at the entrance to the administration building

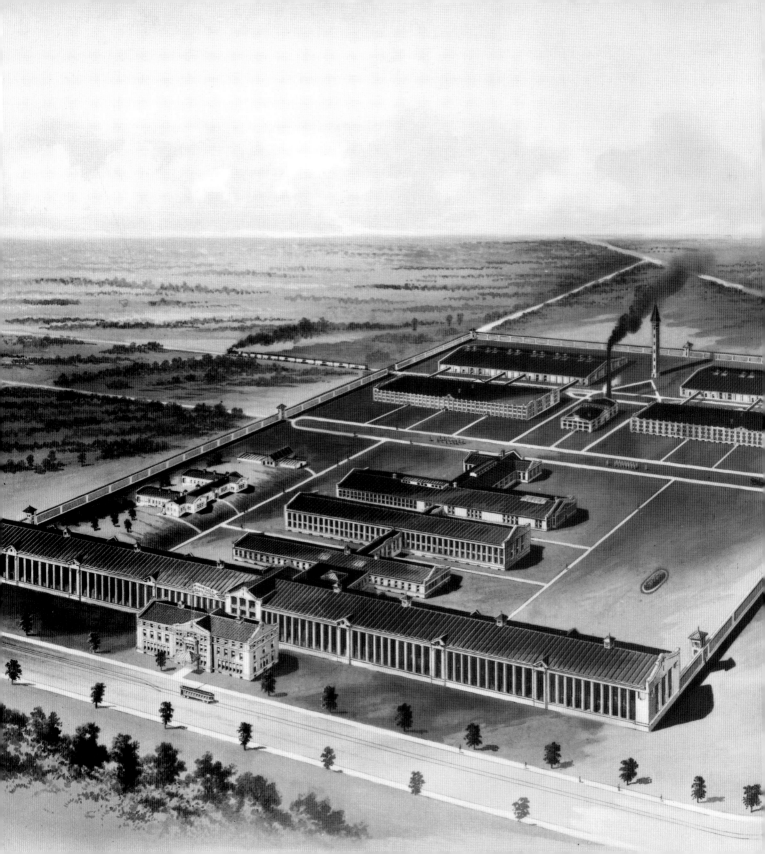

The New Era

Warden Henry Wolfer

In October 1914, with his dream of a new prison realized, Wolfer invited many of his old friends to tour the facility, then announced his intention to retire from his position as warden. In his final report to the prison board of managers, he reflected on all the changes that had occurred during the years the old prison was in operation.

The new prison is now completed, and as you know, it is pronounced the last word on all points by the best judges on prison requirements. Prison reform has long been one of the unsolved problems of our civilization. Our new prison not only enables us to put into practical use the best educational and reformative measures, but will provide adequately for the trying out of new ideas and theories, having in mind the rescue and betterment of the unfortunate inmate. After all, this is the only permanent safeguard to society. He must be saved if possible. If he is so morally and mentally twisted that he cannot be eventually restored to his place in society then he must be saved from himself, in order that he may neither destroy himself or harm society.

Social science is wrestling with this subject as never before. While we have made good strides in solving some of the modern prison problems I would say that there is very much yet to be learned, many unsolved problems. May God grant to our faithful workers unfailing patience, practical enthusiasm, and much confidence in the saving power of our Creator and the dictates of humanity.

An artist's conception of the completed prison about 1912

As this is my last report may I be permitted to briefly outline some changes that have come about during the past forty-three years, covered by my prison experience. In the earlier years prisons were unsanitary and badly kept. Filth and squalor was the rule and well organized government unknown. Then, brute force was the rule and rebellion the shibboleth. Society looked upon the criminal as a willful, vicious, untamed brute who needed only punishment and lots of it. Society was responsible to a certain degree for the low ideals of prison management. Times have since changed and we have changed much in Minnesota.

Twenty-four years ago all our inmates worked under contract at 50 cents per day under unsanitary conditions; few privileges were allowed; no amusements; no recreation. All wore stripes; marched in lock step; and all reduced to the dead level of hopeless mediocrity. Nothing to encourage ambition or enlist initiative. There was a large deficit every year which the taxpayers of the state were called upon to make good. In spite of the hard conditions the inmate earned only enough to pay about one-half the expenses of his keep. Minnesota has since not only solved the economic side of our prison problem, but she has also gone well to the front in providing means to rehabilitate her unfortunate members. Today she has one of the best prisons in the world and enough money has already been made by and through her industries to pay for it. The institution has long since ceased to be a burden to the taxpayers, while it has done much to elevate and reform its inmates.

CLOSING THE OLD PRISON
George L. Bartlett, #4342

When the old prison gates were closed, there were eight prisoners left, because of certain legal technicalities that required a "prison to be maintained in the City of Stillwater." Martin Powers was placed in full charge of these men, occupying the rather unique position of Guard, Keeper, Deputy Warden, and Warden, of a prison all his own.

LEVELED AND SCATTERED

The new prison that Henry Wolfer envisioned and saw built became a model for prisons around the country and remains the Minnesota State Prison to this day. In time, as Stillwater grew to the south and annexed South Stillwater, now called Bayport, the people of Minnesota once again began to refer to doing hard time simply as being "sent to Stillwater."

Meanwhile, the old prison stood abandoned on the north edge of town. The former shops were leased first to the American Motor Company as a foundry to make auto parts, then taken over during the 1920s by the Twin City Forge and Foundry, which knocked down the east-facing main wall for easier access. When the

Depression hit, the shops sat empty and the state had to decide what would become of the old prison.

Officials chose to save the shops, because they could be used later—and indeed were used for war production during World War II. In 1936, as part of a WPA project, the main buildings were torn down and the stones scavenged for riprap to slow erosion along the Mississippi River from St. Paul to Red Wing.

In 1941 Governor Harold Stassen signed the warden's house over to the Washington County Historical Society for use as a museum.

WPA workers take a break from the demolition of the prison buildings, 1936

Notes

Notes on the Introduction

The portrait of Henry Wolfer on page 21 appears courtesy Washington County Historical Society. All other photographs are from the collections of the Minnesota Historical Society (MHS).

1. Minnesota Territory, *House Journal,* 1849, p. 16, 17; 1851, p. 23.

2. Minnesota Territory, *Laws,* 1851, p. 5.

3. Bonds dated July 16, 1851, and May 4, 1852, in "Miscellaneous Papers, 1849–1858," Secretary of State's Papers; Board of Inspectors of the Territorial Prison of Minnesota Territory and the State Prison, "Record of Proceedings," February 4, 1853, in Minnesota State Archives; Minnesota Territory, *Laws,* 1853, p. 10.

4. *Daily Minnesota Pioneer* (St. Paul), December 27, 1854; *House Journal,* 1854, p. 44–54.

5. "Personal Record of Warden," March 17, April 30, October 17, November 10, December 11, 1856, in Minnesota State Prison archives, Bayport. The prison records cited in this introduction were made available to the writer in 1960 through the courtesy of Warden Douglas C. Rigg and members of his staff.

6. Minnesota, *General Laws,* extra session, 1857, p. 188; Minnesota Territorial Prison, *Fifth Annual Report,* 9.

7. Territorial Prison, *Fifth Annual Report,* 6.

8. *Weekly Pioneer and Democrat* (St. Paul), December 3, 1857; Territorial Prison, *Fifth Annual Report,* 7, 14; Joint Committee of the Legislature, *Report,* 1858.

9. In 1862 Delano was elected mayor of Stillwater, and after his term in office he moved to St. Paul to become general superintendent of the St. Paul and Pacific Railway. The town of Delano was named in his honor. See Warren Upham and Rose B. Dunlap, *Minnesota Biographies,* 172 (*Minnesota Historical Collections,* vol. 14).

10. Letters of 1858, printed as *Stillwater Prison, Official Correspondence,* and bound with the Minnesota Historical Society's copy of the prison's *Annual Reports.*

11. "Record of Warden," August 28, September 23, 1858.

12. Board of Inspectors, "Proceedings," August 19, 1858; *Stillwater Messenger,* February 21, 1885. Edward Eggleston was prison chaplain from July 1 to September 30, 1861.

13. *Messenger,* February 21, 1885; "Record of Warden," December 28, 1859; Minnesota State Prison, *Annual Report* to the legislature of 1859–60, p. 5.

14. Minnesota, *General Laws,* 1862, p. 133; 1874, p. 132.

15. "Record of Warden," August 26, 1858; State Prison, *Annual Report* to the legislature of 1860–61, p. 4; to the legislature of 1863, p. 26; *Stillwater Democrat,* February 4, 1860.

16. State Prison, *Annual Report* to the legislature of 1859–60, p. 3; to the legislature of 1862, p. 4; *Democrat,* January 19, 1861; *Taylor's Falls Reporter,* June 19, 1869.

17. State Prison, *Annual Report* to the legislature of 1869, p. 7; John W. McClung, *Minnesota as It Is in 1870,* 269 (St. Paul, 1870); *Messenger,* August 9, 1872.

18. *St. Paul Dispatch,* quoted in *Messenger,* February 27, 1874; State Prison, *Annual Report* to the legislature of 1873, p. 4.

19. State Prison, *Biennial Report* to the legislature of 1883, p. 6; *North Western Manufacturing and Car Company,* 3 (1882); Special Committee of the House of Representatives, Appointed to Investigate the Conduct and Management of the State Prison at Stillwater, *Report,* 10 (St. Paul, 1891); Seymour, Sabin and Company, Minute Book February 15, 1882, owned by the

Minnesota Historical Society (MHS).

20. State Prison, *Biennial Report*, 1884, p. 7.

21. Special Committee of the House, *Report*, 2, 12, 20.

22. George B. Engberg. "The Knights of Labor in Minnesota," *Minnesota History*, 22 (December 1941): 387.

23. Blake McKelvey, *American Prisons*, 103 (Chicago, 1936).

24. State Prison, *Annual Report* to the legislature of 1866, p. 3; to the legislature of 1868, p. 4.

25. *Stillwater Republican*, September 27, 1870; *St. Paul Pioneer*, September 1, 1870.

26. *Pioneer*, August 26, 28, 1870; *St. Anthony Falls Democrat*, March 11, 1870; Webber to Austin, August 25, 1870, Pfaender to Austin, September 20, 1870; Jackman to Austin, January 5, 1870, Governors' Archives, in Minnesota State Archives. For biographical information on Webber, see Franklyn Curtiss-Wedge, *History of Freeborn County*, 90, 252, 507 (Chicago, 1911); Edward D. Neill, *History of Freeborn County*, 364 (Minneapolis, 1882).

27. State Prison, *Annual Report* to the legislature of 1872, p. 7; "Punishment Record," August 3, 1872, in Minnesota State Prison archives; *Messenger*, August 9, 1872.

28. *Messenger*, May 22, 1874; *Dispatch*, June 5, 1874; *Pioneer*, January 20, 1874.

29. State Prison, *Biennial Report*, 1884, p. 23–25.

30. State Board of Corrections and Charities, *Biennial Report*, 1886, p. 28.

31. State Prison, *Biennial Report*, 1886, p. 9.

32. John DeLaittre, "Reminiscences," 175, manuscript at MHS.

33. *Messenger*, September 10, 1887.

34. *Messenger*, December 10, 1887; *Prison Mirror* (Stillwater), June 20, 1888.

35. Minnesota, *Laws*, 1889, p. 413–429; Frank Buckley. "Chautauqua in the Minnesota State Prison." *Minnesota History*, 29 (December 1948): 321–333.

36. *Messenger*, October 25, November 15, 1890; Special Committee of the House, *Report*, 28.

37. *Messenger*, December 6, 1890, June 4, 1892; *Prison Mirror*, June 9, 1892.

38. Minnesota, *Laws*, 1893, p. 106–108; 1897, p. 18–20; 1907, p. 58; State Prison, *Biennial Report*, 1894, p. 4.

39. McKelvey, *American Prisons*, 149.

40. "Sent to Stillwater," *Monitor Magazine*, 1 (November, 1911, March, 1912): 50, 214; State Prison, *Biennial Report*, 1902, p. 1; 1904, p. 2; Minnesota, *Laws*, 1905, p. 547; 1909, p. 29; McKelvey, *American Prisons*, 228.

Notes on the Text

Sources are listed below by page numbers. Many of the accounts quoted have been silently edited for length. For full transcriptions, the following original sources should be consulted. Unless otherwise noted, photographs are from the collections of the Minnesota Historical Society (MHS).

Chapter One

23 "Through the Gates" appeared as "Fresh Fish" in *Thru the Mill* (St. Paul, 1915), 8–11, written anonymously by "4342." Convict number 4342 was George L. Bartlett; copyright for *Thru the Mill* was registered to G. L. Bartlett. Lock from MHS collections; photograph by Peter Latner.

27 *Handbook of the Minnesota State Prison* (Stillwater, 1909), 3–4.

31 Bartlett, *Thru the Mill*, 12–19. In the original text, Murphy is identified only as "M——." He has been identified by comparing internal evidence with the convict record.

39 Heilbron, *Convict Life at the Minnesota State Prison* (St. Paul, 1909), 16–23.

40 Drawings of Bertillon method from *Convict Life at the Minnesota State Prison*, 17–21.

41 Compass and caliper courtesy Washington County Historical Society; photographs by Eric Mortenson.

43 Mug shot camera courtesy Washington County Historical Society; photograph by Eric Mortenson.

47 *Handbook of the Minnesota State Prison* (1903), 10–11.

48 Phillips, "Sent to Stillwater," *Monitor Magazine* 2 (April 1912): 30.

Chapter Two

53 Cole Younger, *The Story of Cole Younger by Himself* (Chicago: Press of the Henneberry Co., 1903; St. Paul: MHS Press, 2000), 86–88.

54 Handcuffs courtesy of Bob Davis; photograph by James Jasek.

57 F. P. L., "A Day in Our Prison," *Prison Mirror* (Stillwater), August 31, 1887.

61 Beaudry, "Recollections—Sad and Pleasant," *Prison Mirror*, December 18, 1887; Beaudry, "Died," *Prison Mirror*, January 18, 1888.

65 This version of Younger's account of the prison fire is derived from *Convict Life at the Minnesota State Prison* (St. Paul: Heilbron, 1909; Stillwater: Valley History Press, 1996): 144–147; a shortened version appears in *The Story of Cole Younger by Himself*, 91. Photograph of Abe Hall courtesy Washington County Historical Society.

66 Dodd's account quoted in *The Story of Cole Younger by Himself*, 91; *Third Biennial Report of the Inspectors and Warden of the State Prison to the Governor of Minnesota* (1884), 57–58.

67 Photograph of W. H. Pratt courtesy Washington County Historical Society. Rifle from MHS collections; photograph by Peter Latner.

69 Carter, "Prison Life as I Found It," *Century* 80 (September 1910): 756.

71 Younger, "Some Moralizing by 'Cole,'" *Prison Mirror*, January 18, 1888.

75 "Carter and Price," *Prison Mirror*, April 28, 1910.

76 Heilbron, *Convict Life at the Minnesota State Prison*, 102, 108.

79 *The Story of Cole Younger by Himself*, 91–93.

80 Postmortem photograph courtesy of Steve Amunrud.

83 Knife from MHS collections; photograph by Peter Latner.

85 *Prison Mirror*, August 31, October 19, October 12, 1887; *Stillwater Democrat*, October 13, 1887; November 5, 1887.

89 Turner, "Will a Negro Steal?" *Prison Mirror*, October 12, 1887.

91 Jones, "Race Love—'Will a Negro Steal?'" *Prison Mirror*, October 19, 1887. For Turner's reply to Jones's article, in which he accused Jones of "unsophisticated negroism," see "Plain Black and White," *Prison Mirror*, October 26, 1887.

93 Bartlett, *Thru the Mill*, 48–49.

94 Turner, "The Dungeon," *Prison Mirror*, November 23, 1887.

Chapter Three

99 Phillips, "Sent to Stillwater," *Monitor Magazine* 1 (October 1911): 30; *Stillwater Daily Gazette*, September 9, 1896; "Two Prison Guard with Total Service of 97 Years Retired Under State Law," *Stillwater Daily Gazette*, July 2, 1935.

100 Photograph of Rogan from "He Is a Bad Man," *Minneapolis Tribune*, June 17, 1900.

101 Photograph of Martin Powers courtesy of William Powers. Photographer unknown, probably John Runk.

103 *Eighth Biennial Report of the Inspectors and Warden of the State Prison to the Governor of Minnesota* (1894), 13.

105 All accounts of the twine shop insurrection are drawn from interviews contained in the Stillwater State Prison collection, Minnesota State Archives at MHS.

108 *The Story of Cole Younger by Himself*, 93–100.

111 *Eighth Biennial Report of the Inspectors and Warden of the State Prison to the Governor of Minnesota* (1896), 55.

113 "Escaped from State Prison," *Stillwater Daily Gazette*, March 6, 1911.

114 "Dying Robber Murders Slayer," *Minneapolis Journal*, July 16, 1911.

115 "Shoots Captor on Car," *Minneapolis Journal*, August 13, 1911. Upon his capture, Juhl gave the false name John Lewis, thus "Juhl" has been silently substituted for "Lewis" throughout this account. "Detective Dies; Juhl His Slayer," *Minneapolis Journal*, August 14, 1911.

117 Phillips, "Sent to Stillwater," *Monitor Magazine* 1 (October 1911): 26–31.

121 Phillips, "Sent to Stillwater," *Monitor Magazine* 1 (December 1911): 90.

123 Carter, *Hard Labor and Other Poems* (Boston, 1910), 1.

124 Phillips, "Sent to Stillwater," *Monitor Magazine* 1 (November 1911): 59–60.

125 Phillips, "Sent to Stillwater," *Monitor Magazine* 1 (January 1912): 140.

126 Phillips, "Sent to Stillwater," *Monitor Magazine* 1 (January 1912): 138.

127 For a full account of Sussman's trial, see Paul D. Nelson, *Fredrick L. McGhee: A Life on the Color Line, 1861–1912* (St. Paul: MHS Press, 2002), 177–178.

129 *Handbook of the Minnesota State Prison* (1909), 5–6, 11–12.

133 "Ho for the New Prison," *Prison Mirror*, January 28, 1909.

139 *Eighteenth Biennial Report of the Inspectors and Warden of the State Prison to the Governor of Minnesota* (1914), 1–2.

140 Bartlett, *Thru the Mill*, 62.

141 Heilbron, *Convict Life at the Minnesota State Prison*, 160–165.

Index